PUSHING THE RIVER

PUSHING THE RIVER

An Epic Battle, a Lost History, a Near Death, and Other True Canoeing Stories

FRANK BURES

Foreword by Alex Hutchinson

MINNESOTA HISTORICAL SOCIETY PRESS

Pushing the River was designed and set in type
by Judy Gilats in St. Paul, Minnesota. The text typeface
is Fairplex Wide Medium designed by Zuzana Licko.
The display face is Field Gothic designed by Max Phillips.

mnhspress.org @mnhspress

The Minnesota Historical Society Press is a member
of the Association of University Presses.

Manufactured in the United States of America

10 9 8 7 6 5 4 3 2 1

♾ The paper used in this publication meets the minimum requirements of the American National Standard for Information Sciences—Permanence for Printed Library Materials, ANSI Z39.48-1984.

International Standard Book Number
ISBN: 978-1-68134-312-9 (paper)
ISBN: 978-1-68134-313-6 (e-book)

Library of Congress Control Number: 2024948472

For Hunter Smoak and Jake Abrahams

CONTENTS

THE LOST HISTORY OF THE PAUL BUNYAN CANOE DERBY

JOURNEYS

ADVENTURERS

THE RACE FOR THE RECORD

FOREWORD

In 1944, Pierre Trudeau—then a young university student, later the "philosopher king" who served as prime minister of Canada for sixteen years in the 1960s, '70s, and '80s—wrote a famous essay in which he drew a distinction between "canoeing" and "going on a canoe expedition." Puttering around a local pond is lots of fun, he acknowledged, but only by pushing onward for days or weeks or even months at a time can you reap the full harvest.

"What sets a canoeing expedition apart is that it purifies you more rapidly and inescapably than any other," he wrote. "Travel a thousand miles by train and you are a brute; pedal five hundred on a bicycle and you remain basically a bourgeois; paddle a hundred in a canoe and you are already a child of nature."

Trudeau's convictions were formed on a five-hundred-mile voyage from Montreal up the Ottawa River to James Bay that he undertook with a friend when he was twenty-two. For Frank Bures, his crucible is the Mississippi River, on whose banks he grew up and where he still lives and paddles. In the pages that follow, you'll read about voyages both recent and long-ago, urban and wild, successful and disastrous, by Bures and by many others. There are a million ways to see the world from a canoe. But what unites these stories is that the canoe becomes more than a flotation device; it becomes a vehicle of self-discovery in which the paddlers, as Trudeau advised, "resolve to reach the saturation point."

I realize this may sound offputtingly hardcore. My friends and I have spent many an evening around the campfire debating the precise ratio of suffering to pleasure that makes for a great canoe trip. I recall with great fondness long-ago trips with overly ambitious itineraries that left us hunting for campsites by flashlight, shoveling in handfuls of gorp for dinner, then collapsing into a dreamless sleep in our ancient hand-me-down sleeping bags. But I don't have any particular desire to reenact those sufferfests.

These days, I like aiming to camp by 3:00 or 4:00 PM, early enough to get in a nice swim, maybe catch a fish or two, and explore my surroundings—but with the reassuring knowledge that at least once on every trip, enough things will go wrong that we'll end up with a longer push. I like to think that I'm not just older now, but also wiser, recognizing that it's not about suffering for the sake of suffering. It's about taking on enough of a challenge to strip away the extraneous trappings of modern life. "The residue of our lives—the phone calls, the emails, the deadlines—seemed to trail behind us in the water," Bures writes of one trip. "But with every mile, these drifted farther away."

This is the feeling we chase when we step into a canoe, push off from the shore, and take those first tentative paddle strokes. But if you can't be on the water, the next best thing is to be reading about it—marveling at the racing prowess of Gene Jensen and the Tibbetts family, shivering as Bures capsizes into hypothermic spring waters, or drifting with the Mississippi's current on a homeward pilgrimage. Enjoy the voyage!

Alex Hutchinson
Toronto, October 2024

INTRODUCTION

Sometime in the 1960s, an old canoe washed up on the shore of Minnehaha Creek, across the water from my grandmother's house west of Minneapolis. The family kept an eye on it for a few days, and when no one came to claim it, they floated it over to her yard. It's been in our family ever since.

My grandma wasn't much of an outdoorswoman, so we took the canoe to our home in Winona. In the years since, I've paddled it countless times—on the Mississippi River, through the Boundary Waters, and up and down Lake Winona. Between that old tank and other newer boats, canoeing has woven through much of my life, and I've come to think of the canoe as the perfect vehicle: in it, you almost become part of the water, part of the wild, moving through it on nothing but your own power. As Sigurd Olson once wrote, "Should you be lucky enough to be moving across a calm surface with mirrored clouds, you may have the sensation of suspension between heaven and earth, of paddling not on the water, but through the skies themselves."

Canoeing can be a serene paddle across the sky, but it can also be a test of what's at your core. Part of the allure of paddling the Mississippi is that despite the dams, despite the houses and docks along the shore, it still feels like the same river canoes have been traveling for millennia. The river is still a wild, unpredictable, and sometimes dangerous place, as it has been since it first started to flow. When we dip our paddles into its water today, we are dipping into that deeper time. And when we test ourselves in a canoe, we can be measured against all the paddlers who came before us. The river flows, but in pushing the river we find out what we're made of.

This book is a journey through history, through fire, through cold, and down the Mississippi River, which connects the city where I live now with the one where I grew up. Because we lived on the river, there was always adventure waiting right in our backyard. When I asked the legendary canoeist Bob O'Hara why he loved canoeing, he told me, "There's always something new around the corner. That's why you go. It's always so different. Your mind's always working. It's just a sense of perpetual adventure."

That's what I love about setting off in a canoe. And while today I live further north and on a different stretch of the Minnehaha Creek than my grandma, that old Grumman still sits in our backyard, waiting for its next ride.

So whether you're yearning for a quiet day paddling on a calm lake or you want to push the river, let's hit the water and see what's around the bend.

THE LOST HISTORY

of the

PAUL BUNYAN CANOE DERBY

A RACE AND A RESCUE

1949

IN THE EARLY MORNING HOURS OF SATURDAY, JULY 16, 1949, eighteen-year-old Billy Smith Jr. and his partner Bob Bergstrom, a speed skater in his early thirties, settled into their canoe and started paddling across Lake Winnibigoshish, a reservoir on the Mississippi River in north-central Minnesota. At sixteen miles across, it's one of the most dangerous stretches on the Upper Mississippi River.

The two were racing in the 450-mile Paul Bunyan Aquatennial Canoe Derby from Bemidji to Minneapolis. Of the forty-nine teams that left Bemidji the day before, only thirty-four would remain by the end of Saturday.

When Smith and Bergstrom started across, the lake was calm. "Once we got out on the water, the wind picked up and it got pretty wavy," says Smith, at ninety-three, in an interview at his small home in Shorewood, Minnesota.

Water washed over their gunnels. The boat began to fill. "Before the race started," Smith says, "I noticed the experienced paddlers had coffee cans in their boats. I thought they were for peeing, but I found out the hard way it was for bailing. So we just slowly sank."

The two were in the water, hanging on to the swamped canoe, when a small motorboat came skimming across the lake. Piloting it was Jesse Tibbetts, a fifty-six-year-old Ojibwe former canoe racer from Ball Club, Minnesota, a small town on the Mississippi that, like

Lake Winnibigoshish, sits within the Leech Lake Reservation. "He came bouncing on top of these waves. Then he came over, picked up our canoe, and dumped out the water. We said, 'Thank you,' and we took off. He saved the day for us."

It was the second time in two days that Smith and Bergstrom had been saved by Ojibwe paddlers. The day before, after the race had started on Lake Bemidji, they got stranded in the middle. "I was so excited," Smith says, "that I broke two paddles on Lake Bemidji. And I was sitting there with my partner Bob."

Then along came two other racers, brothers Jim and Bernie Smith (no relation to Billy Smith), also Ojibwe men from Ball Club, Minnesota. This was their fourth derby, and they had placed in the top five in every race so far. They pulled up next to Billy Smith Jr. and threw him a paddle. "Here," one of them said. "Use this."

Billy noticed right away that the paddle was different. "It was an interesting design," he says. "It was shorter with a very thick grip—almost twice of what you see now. But there was no slippage."

The three Smiths already knew each other. In fact, Bill Smith was actually paddling the canoe Jim and Bernie had used in the previous year's race. Now they'd gone above and beyond. They had even gone against their own interests. "I never quite understood why they'd do that," says Smith, "because it cost them a place, which was important to them financially. But even when we came in that day, who was waiting for me but Jim and Bernie Smith? They shook my hand. I wasn't even out of the boat yet, and they said I could keep the paddle. It was a homemade paddle that they used. And that's when I decided: These guys are my friends."

It wouldn't be a good year for Jim and Bernie Smith, who dropped out at Aitkin, less than halfway through the race. But Billy Smith and Bob Bergstrom would finish fourth overall, winning $750 (nearly $10,000 in today's dollars), enough for Billy to pay for a year of college at the University of Minnesota.

The 1949 race was the biggest and richest Paul Bunyan Canoe Derby yet. It was the seventh time the race had been run since starting in 1940, and it attracted competitors from across the United States and Canada.

The canoe derby started in 1940, and it was conceived as a grand event leading up to the Minneapolis Aquatennial celebration. For more than a week, teams would paddle a section of the river, stay overnight, then start again the next morning. Each team's time for the lap would be recorded, and the race standings were then calculated every night.

In the morning, the canoes lined up on the shore, and the teams were released at one- or two-minute intervals in reverse order of their finish the night before. The last canoe went out first. The previous day's first-place paddlers started last and had to chase everyone else down.

The race began in Bemidji near the Paul Bunyan statue. On many years the race's start took place during the city's Paul Bunyan celebration, which went by various names. The day before the derby, there was always a short sprint race, usually one mile long, on Lake Bemidji.

After eight or nine days (depending on how the stages were divided) the racers arrived in Minneapolis. The final lap ended just above St. Anthony Falls. After that, the canoes were trucked or portaged around the falls to the East River Flats below the University of Minnesota, where a final sprint race to the Franklin Avenue Bridge was launched. The finish of the race marked the start of the Aquatennial.

After ten days of breathless race reporting on radio stations and front-page coverage in newspapers, enormous crowds, ranging from 10,000 to 100,000 spectators, turned out to watch the finish. The race brought an awareness of the Mississippi, of the towns along the way, and of canoeing as both adventure and a sport to countless Minnesotans. The derby tapped into, and deepened our love affair with the canoe.

The Paul Bunyan Canoe Derby was the first and longest race of its kind: only Quebec's La Classique Internationale de Canots de la Mauricie (the Mauricie International Canoe Classic), a three-day, 120-mile race that began in 1934, is older. It was also the richest canoe race in North America, with the total purse reaching $10,000 in later years—well over $100,000 in today's dollars.

The derby also launched the modern era of canoe racing in North America. It was there that canoeing legends like Gene Jensen, Irwin "Buzzy" Peterson, Karl Ketter, and Tom Estes all got their start.

Yet the derby was something else too. In the early days, many of the top competitors were from Ojibwe (also known as Anishinaabe or Chippewa) communities of northern Minnesota. Their relatives had been plying those same waters for hundreds of years, using canoeing traditions that go back millennia.

The canoe derby was a rare neutral ground where white and Native outdoorsmen could compete on an even field, exchanging knowledge and ideas and the occasional paddle. As they made their way downstream, they developed friendships and rivalries and connections that would last long after they crossed the finish line. It was an event that blurred some of the painful divides in our culture and history, as the men (and a few women) raced down the river in pursuit of glory and riches.

The long shadow of the Paul Bunyan Canoe Derby is known to many in the canoeing community. But even there, the history of the derby, with its pain, heroism, and brilliance, has nearly been lost. And few are aware of the longer history from which the derby emerged.

PADDLING THROUGH HISTORY

IN THE SUMMER OF 2021, TAMARA THOMSEN WAS SCUBA DIVing in the southwest corner of Lake Mendota, in Madison, Wisconsin. Thomsen, a maritime archaeologist, specialized in studying Great Lakes shipwrecks for the Wisconsin Historical Society. But on this day, she and a friend were diving for fun. They had diver propulsion vehicles—a kind of underwater scooter—and their only plan was to "chase fish and pick up trash."

Just as their air was about to run out, they spotted what looked like a dugout canoe sticking out of the sediment. It was twenty-seven feet below the surface, not far from the affluent suburb of Shorewood Hills. On top of the canoe was a pile of rocks.

Thomsen took out her underwater notebook and scribbled "Dugout canoe." Later that day, she came back to investigate it further and found that it was intact. She covered it up again to help preserve it and marked the spot with GPS.

It took some time to consult with leaders of the Ho-Chunk Nation and the Bad River Band of Lake Superior Chippewa, then to organize an excavation of the fragile craft. But that fall they brought the canoe out of the water. Carbon dating showed that it was twelve hundred years old, carved from an ash tree. The rocks were "net sinkers" used for fishing.

The following spring, Thomsen was teaching a scuba diving class in the same area when she spotted another canoe: this time, a three-thousand-year-old dugout, carved from a single piece of white oak. This too was removed from the lake.

Then in January of 2023, when Lake Mendota was frozen, archaeologists crisscrossed the area with ground-penetrating radar and identified eleven more canoes. They concluded that the area must have been an ancient shoreline, and that these canoes were cached underwater to preserve them through the winter. For some reason, they had been forgotten, discarded, or lost.

That summer, samples were taken from the other canoes. The youngest was found to be eight hundred years old; the oldest, made from elm, was forty-five hundred years old. Others were carved from cottonwood and red oak.

At a time when the great pyramids of Egypt were being built, as Stonehenge was being erected, and while civilization was just taking root in Mesopotamia, canoes were being carved and paddled throughout the waters of our region.

In Minnesota in the 1960s, when rivers and lakes were low, dugout canoes were found throughout southern Minnesota and along the Minnesota River. These included the Bloomington canoe (which dates to about 1820), the Minnesota River canoe (mid-1600s), the Chippewa River canoe (1500), and the Lake Minnetonka canoe (estimated at nearly a thousand years old). But the Lake Mendota canoes show there are almost certainly more canoes hidden deep in our lakes and rivers.

Dugout canoes were used well into the modern era, especially by Dakota people. The makers built controlled fires in a log, dowsed the flames, and scraped out the charred wood to shape the canoe. But around three thousand years ago, a new technology started to emerge. That's when tools for dugout construction started being replaced with the tools for making bark canoes in the Eastern Woodlands.

Bark canoes can be made from elm, chestnut, spruce, cedar, hickory, basswood, or cottonwood. The bark is stretched over a wooden frame, sewn together, and waterproofed with pitch. But bark from those trees has rough surfaces that need to be scraped off before they can be used. The best bark for canoes, by far, comes from the paper birch tree. Since birchbark canoes don't last forty-five hundred years, no matter how they're cached, their history remains opaque.

The first European reference to bark canoes was in 1535 from Jacques Cartier, who saw two such canoes carrying seventeen men. They were also described in 1603 by Samuel de Champlain, the governor of New France, who reported the boats were between twenty and twenty-three feet long and could carry half a ton. He wrote that his fully manned longboat was passed by two bark canoes, each with just two paddlers.

That same year, Captain George Weymouth saw bark canoes off the shore of Maine and was impressed by their speed and craftsmanship. Some bark canoes were said to be thirty or even forty feet long, with a hull an eighth of an inch thick.

In the 1600s, when Ojibwe people began arriving in Minnesota, pushed by European colonists and pulled west by prophesy, they brought their lighter, faster canoes. As Edwin Adney and Howard Chappelle wrote in *Bark Canoes and Skin Boats of North America*, "All the important bands within the [Ojibwe] tribal group were expert canoemen and builders."

Different groups preferred different models, like the "high-end canoe" and the "long-nose canoe," as well as canoes for different purposes, like hunting, portaging, fishing, and hauling freight.

Some Dakota groups did use birchbark canoes for ricing, but little is known about their methods, and many Dakota also used dugouts. According to historian Anton Treuer, this was to the Ojibwe's benefit. "When war broke out between the two tribes in the middle of the 1700s," he writes, "the Ojibwe had a major technological advantage over the Dakota because of canoes and geography. The Dakota used wooden dugouts and had to paddle upstream to attack Ojibwe villages. The Ojibwe would typically rally their warriors and pursue the Dakota, easily overtaking them in faster birchbark canoes. When the Ojibwe attacked the Dakota, they would float downstream for a couple of days, strike, and flee in their faster craft. From 1600 to 1825, the Ojibwe multiplied the size of their territory twentyfold at the expense of other tribes."

The French and other fur traders saw the advantage of the birchbark canoe right away. Adney and Chappelle wrote that "The speed with which they could be propelled by the Indians also caused amazement, as did their light weight and marked strength, combined with a great load-carrying capacity." Champlain was the first to argue that bark canoes would be necessary to penetrate the backcountry of North America.

By the mid-1800s, demand for canoes among white people was growing fast, and a number of companies, like the Peterborough Canoe Company in Ontario, were founded. These companies' early canoes were based on dugouts, but they later switched to "cedar strip," canoes with ribs covered in wood or canvas. These were based on birchbark models and forms.

"The wooden canoes were completely based on Native American designs," says Mark Neuzil, author of *Canoes: A Natural History in North America*. "In fact, the molds they use were based on either Huron or Cree, the tribes around Peterborough. So that became the basis for many of the wood and canvas models like Old Town, Chestnut, and Peterborough. The basic shape is Native American, but it's not a coastal native canoe. It's more Ojibwe, Cree, or Huron."

This combination of Native knowledge and industrial production turned the canoe into a North American icon, and something that can be found in millions of backyards across the northern United States and Canada.

Not only did the canoe provide a way of life for Native people, fuel the fur trade, and open up vast expanses to European exploration, it also launched a love affair with the craft that would lay the groundwork for the Paul Bunyan Canoe Derby.

EARLY CANOE RACES

1910–1914

DOCUMENTATION OF EARLY CANOE RACING IN MINNESOTA IS hard to come by. Calls to tribal historic preservation offices and other historians around the state yielded just two photographs from June 1910 labeled "Indian canoe race, White Earth, Minn." An article about the 1941 Paul Bunyan Canoe Derby reported, "In ninth were the noted veteran paddlers Jess and Jim Tibbetts, who have been competing in canoe races for over 40 years."

What those races—dating back to 1900—might have been we may never know. But according to Wayne Valliere of the Lac du Flambeau Band of Lake Superior Chippewa in Wisconsin (one of just six master birchbark canoe builders in the Midwest), his band has records of canoe races from the early 1900s and through today. He says they're typically sprints in the one-mile range, but they can span the length of Lac du Flambeau, up to twenty-five miles. He believes most Ojibwe communities held races. "Anishinaabe are a very competitive people," Valliere says. "We had lacrosse. We had the snow snake game. And canoes were a huge part of our culture. They carried everything. So you can bet that if we had them, we raced them."

There is more evidence of early racing of wood or wood-and-canvas canoes among white Minnesotans. In the summer of 1912, for example, competitions on the Chain of Lakes in Minneapolis

Ojibwe men race at White Earth, Minnesota, 1910. *Northwest Minnesota Historical Center, Minnesota State University Moorhead*

included a series of "war canoe" races, with twelve paddlers to a canoe, along with a host of other races: 100-yard singles, 200-yard doubles, an "overboard contest," where competitors "paddle a certain distance, jump overboard, reclaim their canoes and finish the race." There were also a "standing canoe race" and a contest where racers paddled with their hands, not to mention a "tilting contest," a ladies' war canoe race, and a "peewee" canoe race. There was even an event in which the bow and stern paddlers had to switch places at the sound of a pistol shot.

By 1913, the region was filled with canoe clubs, including the Harriet Canoe Club, the Minnesota River Canoe Club, the Lake Phelan Canoe Club, the Duluth Boat Club, the Como Canoe Association, and others.

In September of 1913, these groups banded together to form the Northwest Canoe Association. That same month, the Minnesota River Canoe Club held a twenty-five-mile canoe marathon on the Minnesota River that went from Savage to Fort Snelling. Paddlers left at 2:30 Sunday afternoon. “At what time they will arrive,” the *Minneapolis Morning Tribune* reported, “or to be more exact, just who will arrive, remains to be seen.”

On June 25, 1914, the Minnesota River Canoe Club held a regatta on the Minnesota River. That same year, the Athletic and Boat Club entered five meets and “swept the canoe deck clean,” winning every one.

On Sunday, September 20, 1914, a five-mile canoe race was held on Lake Calhoun (now Bde Maka Ska). “This is the first canoe marathon to be held in the Twin Cities and has aroused considerable interest,” reported the *Minneapolis Sunday Tribune*.

THE MISSISSIPPI MARATHON

1919

FIVE YEARS LATER, MORE INTEREST WOULD BE AROUSED when Minnesota had its first true long-distance canoe race, which took place on the heels of "marathon mania," an era which saw people walking, running, bicycling, and driving hundreds of miles across the country and the world.

On July 3, 1919, paddlers gathered just below the Ford Dam in Minneapolis for the "Mississippi Marathon," in which racers would paddle 133 miles downstream to Winona in a so-called "water marathon."

The race was the brainchild of W. A. Frisbie, editor of the *Minneapolis Daily News* and author of popular children's books like *Mother Goose ABC* and *The Pirate Frog, and Other Tales*. There was no entry fee. The main expense was a $2 railway fare (about $36 today) charged to transport two paddlers and a canoe back to Minneapolis from Winona. Prizes included a $95 Evinrude gasoline canoe motor, a "silver loving cup," an eighteen-foot canoe priced at $75, and a "valuable camp stove." Entrants had to be at least sixteen years old and had to prove they could swim in canoeing clothes.

The *Winona Republican Herald* reported that "Contestants may make a continuous run of it or may camp along shore as they see fit." At the time, there were no dams between Minneapolis and Winona, so there were no portages.

Of the fifty-two teams that registered, only thirty-six started. All canoes carried food and water bottles. One entrant, a certain Charles A. Johnson, had reportedly canoed from Minneapolis to St. Louis five times and knew the river well.

The race started at 11:45 AM. The canoes passed St. Paul before 1:00 PM. That night, the paddlers were hit by a storm on Lake Pepin, and most of them paddled through it. One team capsized twice on Pepin, but managed to get back in their canoe and finished in last place. Another canoe got lost in the backwaters near Wabasha.

The winners, Louis Loughway and Art Hughley of Wabasha, paddled a seventeen-foot Old Town canoe. They passed their hometown at 2:21 AM and arrived in Winona at 7:55 AM. Of the thirty-six teams that started, twenty-two finished. The last-place team arrived just before midnight the same day.

There was talk of making the race an annual event. "Canoe racing is an exciting sport," the *Wabasha Country Herald* wrote, invoking a romanticized version of the area's past, "and in the early days of our history there were many such stirring contests. The Indians and the frontiersmen were adepts in the art of canoeing, and their feats have inspired the muses and live in literature as they do in history."

THE DIAMOND JUBILEE CANOE MARATHON

1928

ALMOST A DECADE LATER, W. A. FRISBIE WAS IN CHARGE OF another race, this one to celebrate seventy-five years since the naming of Minneapolis. As chair of the Diamond Jubilee Outdoor Exposition Committee, he oversaw a canoe race from the Mississippi's source to Minneapolis. The race would be sponsored and run by the Elks Club.

"The decision of the Elks to sponsor the affair," said one report, "was in response to the suggestion of Mayor [George E.] Leach that Minneapolis, gateway to the land of 10,000 lakes, should center attention on the attraction of outdoor Minnesota."

Newspapers reported that the race would be eight hundred miles long, but the actual distance is 491 miles. Organizers debated where the Mississippi River actually starts. Some said it was Lake Itasca; others said Elk Lake, which flows into Lake Itasca. After some debate, Elk Lake was chosen as the start. The race would take thirteen days and would end at the Hennepin Avenue Bridge. The arrival of the canoes in Minneapolis would mark the start of the Diamond Jubilee Outdoor Exposition.

Excitement was high, and not just among paddlers of European descent. The race had a significant number of entrants from Ojibwe communities in northern Minnesota, especially from the town of Ball Club on the Leech Lake Reservation. While much of the news coverage was surprisingly matter-of-fact, it also patronized Ojibwe racers and trafficked in stereotypes. "Indians and half-breeds with their birch bark canoes will compete with their white brothers from all over the state in a test of ability and stamina. Cash prizes totaling $1,000 have been hung up for the winners, with medals and merchandise prizes also to be awarded to other competitors."

The race was a rich affair. First place would receive two diamond-studded medals and $500 (a little over $8,900 in today's dollars); second place got two gold medals and $200; third place received two silver medals and $150; and fourth place got $100.

The race was scheduled to start on Sunday, May 13, at 8:30 AM, "following taking of motion picture scenes and a Chippewa induction ceremony, presided over by Chief [Jim] Greenhill of a tribe of Indians living near Cass Lake."

Nineteen teams showed up at Elk Lake for the start. Another sixteen were not able to make it because of forest fires. Two of the Ojibwe teams (Joe White and Jim Gray, Ben Stewart and Ed Jeremy) arrived with birchbark canoes, but they were not allowed to enter the race. "All four of these men are Chippewa Indians," the *Minneapolis Star* reported. "They were dropped from the derby when the committee decided that their birch bark canoes were not strong enough for the trip. Chief Green Hill of Cass lake, Chippewa tribes offered to get other canoes if the start of the derby could be postponed one day. Because of pre-arranged plans, however, the committee could not consent to this request, and the four Indians dropped out."

(While it's true that birchbark canoes are more easily damaged, master canoe builder Jim Jones of Leech Lake notes that many Native paddlers carried extra bark and resin to make repairs.)

At 10:00 AM fourteen teams set out, leaving two at a time. A few tipped in the rapids. John Wilson (described as "194 pounds and . . . one of the most powerful Indians in the state") and Joe Morgan, Ojibwe paddlers from Ball Club, were in the lead until they punctured their canoe in three places running a rapid. They kept going and still managed to finish fifth for the day.

On day two, they pressed on. Wilson paddled with one hand and bailed with the other. "Despite the fact that the canoe was half filled with water, the team finished in fourth place that night," the paper reported. On the third day, they appealed to the committee to let them replace the canoe, but were denied, so they dropped out.

The first day, Gussie Gustafson and Al Hendrickson, two white paddlers from St. Cloud, were the first team to arrive in Bemidji. But right behind them were four more Native paddlers from Ball Club: Ben Tibbetts and Bill Reynolds, followed by Tommy and Jim Tibbetts—nephews of Ben—in third.

By the end of the second stage, from Bemidji to the edge to Lake Winnibigoshish, Tibbetts and Reynolds moved into the lead, five minutes ahead of second-place Tommy and Jim Tibbetts.

Along the river, thousands of people came out to cheer. Celebrations were held when the contestants reached cities like Grand Rapids, Aitken, and Brainerd, where the teams stayed overnight. As they moved downstream, the Tibbetts brothers held on to second place, while Gustafson and Hendrickson from St. Cloud and Harvey Anderson and Fred Hanson of Mankato vied for third. A couple more teams dropped out, and soon only eleven remained.

Meanwhile, at the front, Bill Reynolds and Ben Tibbetts widened their lead. They paddled one lap, from Brainerd to Aitken, in a little over eight hours, at an average of eleven miles an hour. Tibbetts, forty-eight years old, was Jesse's older brother, and the *Minneapolis Star* noted that their impending victory was due at least in part to the twenty-one-year-old canoe they were paddling, a canoe with a remarkable story: In 1907 Ben Tibbetts had worked as a guide for a man named George Scott on Mud Lake. Scott had paid a canoe builder $160 to make him a canoe especially for that trip. When Tibbetts took the canoe out, he fell in love with it. Every year he looked forward to paddling it when Scott came back. Seeing how much Tibbetts loved the canoe, Scott told him that if he ever got tired of it, or died, Tibbetts could have it.

Scott died in 1920, but Tibbetts heard nothing about the canoe. He started to search for it, asking Scott's relatives where it had ended up. Just twelve days before the 1928 Diamond Jubilee race, he finally found the new owner in Hibbing.

The canoe had passed through eight or nine owners. When Tibbetts got to Hibbing, he told the owner the story. The owner told him if the canoe was damaged, Tibbetts could have it free. If not, the price was $25 (about $450 in current dollars). The canoe was in perfect condition, so Tibbetts bought it and had it shipped to Itasca for the race.

As the paddlers neared Minneapolis, the stakes rose: there was a $50 prize for whoever won the lap from Anoka to Minneapolis. When they came into town on Saturday, May 26, the boats were all stopped at the Camden Bridge for a final sprint.

Downstream, thousands of people packed the Hennepin and Third Avenue Bridges. At 2:30 PM a shout went up: "Here they come!"

Canoe Marathon Finish and Derby Winners

Minneapolis saw the finish of its first canoe derby Saturday, and 22 tired young men, who have been paddling 800 miles in two weeks, welcomed it. At the top, left, are Ben Tibbetts and Bill Reynolds, Chippewa Indians who won the derby. They are being greeted by Mayor Leach. At the right are Gussie Gustafson and Al Hendrickson of St. Cloud, who led the derbyists into Minneapolis, winning the final lap.

At left, the winners of the 1928 Diamond Jubilee canoe marathon, Ben Tibbetts and Bill Reynolds; at right, Al Hendrickson and Gussie Gustafson, fourth-place finishers and winners of the final lap. *Minneapolis Sunday Tribune, May 27, 1928*

The *Minneapolis Sunday Tribune* captured the moment.

> Around the bend in the river two dots swept into view, and the sun flashed on dripping water. They grew larger, took on shape, and were canoes. Just behind them came, two, three, then half a dozen other dots that became canoes. A moment later there were 11 of them, all racing for the finish line, where two flags floated on shore.
>
> Under the main arch of the Hennepin avenue bridge they swept, two craft fighting for the lead. One of them, bright red, with two lads in white shirts, pulling for dear life. The other, a dull green, containing the stolid Chippewas, Tibbetts and Reynolds. Just behind, the rest struggled for position.

Gustafson and Hendrickson, in the red canoe, won the sprint. Ben Tibbetts and Bill Reynolds won the race, with Tom and Jim Tibbetts taking second. Mankato's Harvey Anderson and Fred Hanson came in third.

When the paddlers landed just above St. Anthony Falls, they were surrounded by a crowd. "Everyone wanted to shake the hands of the men who had taken canoeing out of the category of parlor accomplishments and placed it on a par with the 'bunion' derby or a six-day bicycle race—an athletic feat," reported the *Tribune*. (The "Bunion Derby"—the Trans-American Footrace—was a 3,423-mile, eighty-four-day race from Los Angeles to New York, which ended on May 26, the same day as the Diamond Jubilee Marathon.)

The following Wednesday, at 3:30 in the afternoon, there was a "canoe exhibition" in the form of a two-mile race between the winners, Ben Tibbetts and Bill Reynolds, and second-place finishers, Tom and Jim Tibbetts. It started at the Plymouth Avenue Bridge and went just past the Hennepin Avenue Bridge. Tibbetts and Reynolds had to use a borrowed canoe, because theirs was on display at the exposition.

More than five thousand people watched as the canoes battled down the river. Tibbetts and Reynolds led most of the way, sometimes by as much as two canoe lengths. It was estimated they were paddling at nearly fifteen miles per hour.

But after trailing most of the race, the Tibbetts brothers made a final push, closed the gap, and nosed ahead for the win by just sixteen inches. The teams had covered the distance from Plymouth Avenue to Rendell Park (on the east bank at Marquette Avenue, just past the Hennepin Bridge) in eight minutes and thirty-eight seconds.

The entire race was a massive success. and there was talk of making it a yearly contest. One headline said: "Canoe Derby Will Be Made Annual Affair." It was reported there would be $2,000 in prizes in 1929.

It's unclear why there was no derby in the summer of 1929, but with the stock market crash that October, followed by the Great Depression, it would be another twelve years before the race was run again.

THE DAWN OF THE DERBY

1940

BY 1939, PEOPLE WERE READY FOR ANOTHER CANOE RACE. Minneapolis city leaders started planning a celebration for the following year: the Aquatennial. They wanted it to be big, and they wanted it to show off what the city—and the state—had to offer. The kickoff event was to be the Paul Bunyan Aquatennial Canoe Derby, an epic, 450-mile canoe race down the Mississippi River from Bemidji to Minneapolis.

The race would take eight days. At night, paddlers would stop to eat and sleep in towns along the way. Every day along the river, thousands of people would turn out to watch the racers finish and start the next morning. The newspapers wrote breathless race reports—who was winning, who was out, and who was in the running for podium spots and cash, with a total of $1,000 in prize money available, and another $100 for the final sprint into Minneapolis. First place would take home $500—just over $11,000 in today's dollars.

Although it was not explicitly stated, the race was clearly modeled on the 1928 Diamond Jubilee canoe marathon. And like that race, it attracted wide interest among Ojibwe paddlers in northern Minnesota. "Whole Family in Aquatennial Canoe Derby," said one front-page headline in the *Minneapolis Sunday Tribune*. The Tibbetts family had six veterans of the 1928 Diamond Jubilee race, including the winner, Ben Tibbetts.

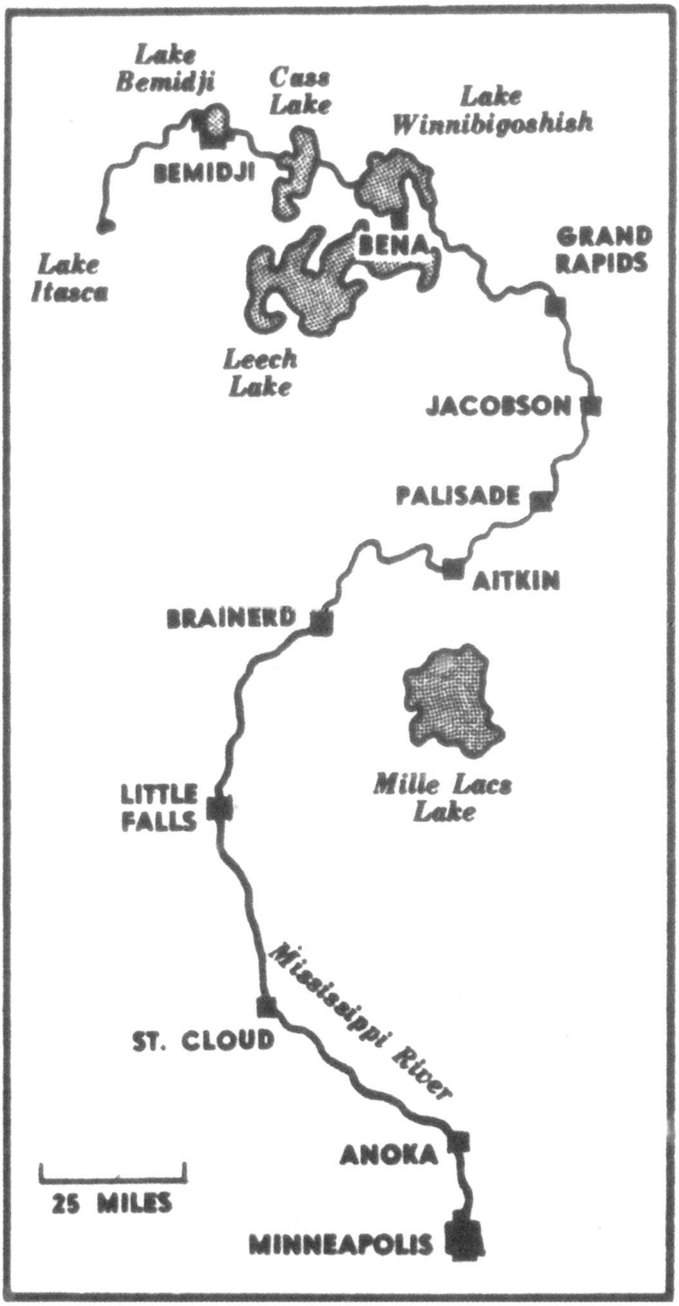

A map of the Paul Bunyan Canoe Derby route, from Bemidji to Minneapolis. *Minneapolis Sunday Tribune, July 12, 1959*

At age sixty, Ben decided to "come out of retirement" and enter the race with his younger brother Jesse Tibbetts, who was forty-seven. There was also Ben's son Marvin (usually called Bud) Tibbetts, with Ben's nephew Harry, and two other nephews of Ben, Tommy and Jim Tibbetts, who had finished second in 1928. The Tibbetts name would be stamped on nearly every canoe derby ever held.

Also returning was John Wilson, who had paddled to fourth place on day two of the 1928 marathon with one hand and three holes in his canoe. Wilson, called Little White Pine, was six foot five and was said to weigh over two hundred pounds. He planned to paddle with his brother, Fred. But for some reason Fred didn't enter, and Wilson ended up partnering with Bill Little Wolf. Elmer Tibbetts, of White Earth, and Bill Fairbanks made up another Native team.

Other 1928 veterans included Harvey Anderson and Fred Hanson of Mankato—the third-place finishers—and Ed Eliason of Hovland, who had been forced to drop out after his canoe got waterlogged crossing Winnibigoshish. When Eliason left the race, he told reporters: "I'll be in the race next year with a real boat, then Ben Tibbetts and all of them will have to watch out." This time he would be racing with his brother Ace Eliason, a former St. Olaf heavyweight boxing champion, and the tables would be turned.

There was another family in the race too: George Messing and his wife Dorothy entered as a team. They were fond of long canoe trips, and had even taken one for their honeymoon. Dorothy Messing was one of only two women ever to enter and finish the Paul Bunyan Canoe Derby.

The start list also said: "Cancelled out was William D. Smith, Minneapolis wrestler, and Fred Otis, Minneapolis truck driver." This was the father of young Billy Smith Jr., who would break two paddles in the 1949 derby. This wouldn't be the elder Smith's last attempt to enter.

* * *

The day before the start of the derby, on Friday, June 12, there was a half-mile sprint race on Lake Bemidji, which Bud and Harry Tibbetts won.

The next day, at 7:30 AM, some twenty-eight teams gathered on the shore of the lake. The judges sent them off across the water at one-minute intervals, so there wouldn't be a jam at the lake's narrow outlet. Not long after they started, however, a strong storm swept over Lake Bemidji and whipped up six-foot waves. Two of the teams tipped and had to be rescued. Another canoe had to be rescued on Cass Lake. (One other canoe was reported missing, but it turned out to belong to two Minneapolis high school students whose mother had refused to sign their consent form, so they never started.)

When the paddlers arrived at the entrance to Lake Winnibigoshish at the end of the first day, Richard and Einar Mattson from Minneapolis were in the lead. Ben and Jesse Tibbetts were less than two minutes behind, and just behind them were Ace and Ed Eliason.

The start of the derby on Lake Bemidji, 1940. *MNHS*

The next day, Lake Winnibigoshish was deemed too rough to cross, "much to the disgust of the various Tibbetts who had expected to profit by their experience in the wild water." Instead, the boats and teams were trucked around it to Grand Rapids.

As they pushed down the river, more teams dropped out. "Back-breaking portages and a blanket of darkness threatened to cut the field drastically in the Minneapolis Aquatennial's Paul Bunyan Canoe derby tonight, as the second day of the race came to a close," the *Minneapolis Morning Tribune* reported.

At Palisade, only ten teams crossed the finish line before dark, with another twelve coming in after nightfall. Five of the top eight teams were Ojibwe racers. Ben and Jesse Tibbetts had fallen back to fourth, while Bud and Harry Tibbetts passed them and moved into third. John Wilson and Bill Little Wolf were in fifth, while Ed and Ace Eliason had surged into first place. Only fourteen minutes separated the first three teams.

As the field narrowed and the stakes rose, conflicts emerged. Anderson and Hanson of Mankato claimed the river wasn't marked, so those who knew it had an advantage. Some teams alleged that "crowding tactics were in vogue."

The weather was also hot, with temperatures passing a hundred degrees. The sun "was like a furnace until the afternoon," said one report. One racer recalled that, because of sunburn, "Ben Tibbetts had skin coming off in handfuls, and Jesse Tibbetts gave everyone a shock when he took off his hat and half the skin on his forehead came with it." Elmer Tibbetts and Bill Fairbanks had to pull over and wait for an hour because Elmer overheated in the blazing sun. Anderson and Hanson dropped out. Tom and Jim Tibbetts did too, after Tom was ill for two days.

But the crowds came out in spite of the heat. When the paddlers arrived in Aitken, some fifteen hundred people greeted the racers. At Brainerd, a local businessman put up money for a sprint, but many of the paddlers declined to race.

They kept pushing downstream. The river was low. The wind was fierce. "Battling a 25-mile-an-hour wind and harassed by stones and shallow water, contestants in the Aquatennial canoe derby pulled wearily into Little Falls tonight. . . . Shallowness of the river made it impossible to dig paddles deeply. Stones caused many near-upsets and the wind, blowing up-river, slowed canoes down and added to the choppiness of the water."

Old Ben and Jesse Tibbetts dropped to seventh place. "Jesse has a very sore arm and a big lump on his shoulder. He traveled in severe pain all day and the wonder is that they did not drop further back," the *Star Journal* reported. Bud and Harry Tibbetts moved into second place. John Wilson and Bill Little Wolf climbed up to fifth place. "Four of the first seven teams are Indians, able to set a fairly fast pace and maintain it all day long," the paper reported.

The race was brutal. Ed Woolverton called each day an "eternity of torture." Einar Mattson, who with his brother was fighting for third place, had over forty blisters on his hands, and "between his fingers and palms was one mass of raw flesh." Mattson's hands were wrapped in a wet, sticky tape. George Faust, the University of Minnesota Gophers football quarterback from 1936 to 1938, dropped out after his partner got stomach cramps. He told the *Star Journal* that the race was "the hardest grind of any sport I know."

Tensions were also rising, and Faust predicted that "There will be some paddle swinging among the teams before it is over." He said some teams were "blocking" other teams for friends in the lead and hiding portage flags, which caused him and his partner to get lost.

Soon they neared Minneapolis, where a massive Aquatennial parade was being planned, with eighty-six "professionally decorated floats." It was reported to be the most floats ever in a single parade in the United States.

On the river, the competition was still tight. Fifteen of the teams were within a half an hour of each other. The Eliason brothers were out front, though the Tibbettses hadn't given up. "Those young Tibbetts boys, Bud and Harry, are fighting grimly for that $500 first prize. They made the fastest lap Thursday even though the tropical sun fairly blistered scalps and made speedy paddling a severe task," reported the paper.

Two handsome brothers, Jesse and LeRoy Goodin, were also moving up in the ranks—from eleventh place to eighth.

On Saturday, the racers arrived in Minneapolis. The final sprint was six miles, from the Camden Bridge to the finish line at the Franklin Avenue Bridge, and it included a portage around St. Anthony Falls. "It was a neck-and-neck finish to a grueling contest that found the contestants worn and weary but undaunted as they struggled over a final portage at St. Anthony falls." The Tibbetts brothers were the first to get to the portage's stairs, which were only big enough for one canoe, giving them a head start on the water below. They won the sprint, along with the extra $50.

Page 8 L MINNEAPOLIS STAR JOURNAL

End of Grueling 450-Mile Aquatennial Canoe Derby

Winner Sprinter

It's end of a long, long paddle for the paddlers shown at the finish line of the final sprint of the Aquatennial Canoe derby that started early in the week from Lake Bemidji. The canoe at the center of the picture, paddled by Bud and Harry Tibbets of Ballclub, Minn., wins the final sprint down river from Camden bridge, and the canoe in the foreground, paddled by Ace and Ed Eliasen of Grand Marais wins the derby. The Tibbets collect $300 for second in the derby and first in the sprint. The Eliasens win $500 for first place in the derby.

Harry and Bud Tibbetts of Ball Club, at back, won the final sprint of the 1940 derby. Ace and Ed Eliason of Hovland, foreground, were the derby's winners. *Minneapolis Star Journal, July 21, 1940*

Ace and Ed Eliason won the derby and $500, followed by Bud and Harry Tibbetts ($250), Art and Henry Eliason ($100), Richard and Einar Mattson ($75), John Wilson and Bill Little Wolf ($50), and another Ojibwe team, James Hunt and Louis Munnell ($25).

The first Paul Bunyan Canoe Derby was a massive success. It was estimated that 100,000 people watched the finish of the race, and another 100,000 spectated in towns along the river

The next year was expected to be bigger and better. The president of the Bemidji Resort Owners Association predicted, "The Paul Bunyan Canoe Derby, in my humble opinion, will become one of the greatest publicity events staged in Minnesota." And the *Minneapolis Star Journal* crowed, "The Aquatennial canoe derby is due to become a national classic."

WHAT IS A CANOE?

1941

IN 1941, THE PAUL BUNYAN CANOE DERBY GENERATED A NEW wave of excitement. It even drew teams from outside Minnesota: one from Chicago and another from Canada. One Minnesota team, Julian Fink and Raymond Kurtz, planned a training trip all the way to New Orleans, starting in April. (There's no record of how far they trained, but they did complete the derby.)

"Bunyan Canoe Course Toughened This Year," read the headline on an article announcing there would be no portage around Lake Winnibigoshish, the most dangerous stretch in the race. Instead, paddlers would have to navigate the lake. "Last year's opening day," the paper reported, "was marred by three capsized crews, two in Bemidji, and one in Cass, and one of the overturned crews narrowly escaped drowning." This year, there would be safety boats on hand.

The 1940 derby winners, Ed and Ace Eliason, opted out of the race in 1941. (Ace had used his prize money to attend the U of M law school.) This made Harry and Bud Tibbetts, who finished second, the favorites. One Ojibwe team from Deer River, Albert Fairbanks and Bob Jackson, couldn't make the start because their canoe fell off a truck on their way to the derby and was damaged.

Yet even without them, ten teams—nearly half the field—came from Ojibwe communities. The *Minneapolis Star Journal* ran a photo of "Bill Reynolds, Indian," weighing in with the headline:

"24 Teams Start on Grueling 450-mile Canoe Derby." (There's no mention of whether he was related to the Bill Reynolds who was the 1928 champion.)

Ed Shave, the outdoors reporter who covered almost every derby for the paper, described the launch on the morning of Saturday, July 5, at the edge of Lake Bemidji. "At 9:16 A.M. Mayor-elect Marvin L. Kline of Minneapolis, fired the starting gun amid the shouts and shrieks of hundreds of spectators lining the banks of picturesque Lake Bemidji." The racers "dipped their paddles and began the 10-day race to Minneapolis. Indians, northwoods guides, trappers and even a bank clerk were among the contestants." The bank clerk was noteworthy, because most of the racers were blue-collar workers: laborers, machinists, farmers, and cement finishers. There were always a few students and office workers, but in general, the derbies were a working-class affair.

The weather was cool, and the water was fast. The first sixteen teams paddled the first lap faster than the previous year's leaders.

The first boat to arrive at the finish on day one carried the Chicago duo of Howie Oslund and Bob Robinson. Oslund was a woodworker and had been canoeing for fifteen years. Robinson was the bank clerk and had been canoeing for nine years. They had raced together as a team for the previous seven years. To train for the derby, they'd practiced for months on Lake Michigan and on the rivers around Chicago. They had also developed a paddling style that, many years later, would be adopted by Olympic canoe sprinters: they knelt on one knee, switching sides every hour. This stance let them use their full upper body, and they claimed it gave them as much distance in one stoke as most people got in three, and about 30 percent more power.

They also had an innovative canoe, eighteen feet long with a thirty-seven-inch beam, weighing eighty-eight pounds. But the other paddlers in the derby didn't like the look of it and didn't think it was even a real canoe. Before the first day was over, a controversy heated up. "A protest was entered against the canoe . . . on the grounds that it was not a canoe but a racing shell"—a craft built for rowing competitions. The head of the derby disagreed. Ed Shave

Chicagoans' Special Canoe Still Paces Derby

Howie Oslund, stern, and Bob Robinson, bow, of Chicago are at present leading the Aquatennial Paul Bunyan canoe derby. Picture shows them in the kneeling position which lets them get the full weight of their body behind each stroke. The canoe in which they are racing has been protested by the other entrants but it has been authorized by the American Canoe association, and was accepted by the Canoe Derby committee.

Howie Oslund and Bob Robinson demonstrated their unusual paddling posture in the canoe that other racers protested, 1941. *Minneapolis Star Journal, July 8, 1941*

reported that it was "a trim canoe built of plywood with tapered hull and rounded bottom."

The Canadian team of Cleo Gaudry and Don Mathieson came in second on the first lap, followed by Dave Clark and Steve Zimmerman, "woods-hardened guides from the Gunflint Trail," who lived in Grand Marais. Zimmerman was also Ojibwe from the Grand Portage Band. Jesse and Jim Tibbetts were behind them in fourth.

The next day, at 4:00 AM, the paddlers started across Lake Winnibigoshish. Apparently no one capsized on the lake, and Harry and Bud Tibbetts were the first to complete the eighty-seven miles to Grand Rapids, eight minutes ahead of the Chicago team.

On the third day, the *Morning Tribune* reported that the paddlers' suffering was starting to show. "With seven days still to go, many contestants, including the leading Chicago team of H. Oslund and Bob Robinson, had to have first aid for badly blistered hands, chafed to the flesh by the thousands of paddle-strokes taken since the derby left Bemidji Saturday. . . . Blisters contributed largely to the troubles of Kenora Ont. team of Mathieson and Gaudry, who fell from second to fourth place yesterday."

Oslund and Robinson won the lap to Jacobson. "Windy City's Tenderfeet Steal Show," read the *Star Journal* headline. "The two Chicago 'tenderfeet' are giving a lot of Minnesota backwoodsmen something to think—and worry—about in the 1941 Minneapolis Aquatennial canoe derby." Oslund and Robinson also got some other good news. A committee had disallowed the protest again them because "while the canoe was unlike any other in the derby, it had the approval of the American Canoe association."

But the other racers weren't about to give up, since there was $1,700 in prize money (around $36,000 in today's dollars) on the line. The next day, when the racers came into Palisade, they filed an official complaint. "Derby 'Trick Canoe' Formally Protested," read the headline. They argued that Oslund and Robinson's boat was not a canoe, but a "special type racing shell." The complaint said: "We fear that this freak type boat, if ruled OK, will cause the end of the derby, as our north woodsmen, using regular canoes, will not be able to compete in future races."

Over a thousand people were waiting for the racers in Palisade, which had a population of two hundred: "Canoe Derbyists Win Wild Welcome at Palisade Stop." The year before had been similar, giving the town a reputation as "the 'hottest' derby town in the state."

When Oslund and Robinson came down the river in first place, locals scratched their heads. "The unorthodox kneeling style of Oslund and Robinson still had observers puzzled," wrote Ed Shave, "but they had to admit it was producing results."

The controversy over the Chicago canoe proved a distraction from the race itself, which was getting interesting. The Canadians had clawed their way back into third place, while two brothers from Crosby-Ironton and Aitken, Walter and Orbid Heineman, had moved up from eighth to sixth. In fact, the Heinemans would be the first canoe on the next two laps, moving up to fifth place overall. "Paddling all day long at a rate of nearly a stroke a second," wrote Ed Shave, "the Heinemans pulled out of sixth place into fifth and was pressing close on fourth place [Harry and Bud Tibbetts] when the lap ended." The Heinemans' stroke rate was counted at 52 to 55 per minute, compared to the average of 38 to 44 per minute. By the time they reached Little Falls, they were in fourth.

The Chicago team beat the Heinemans to Little Falls, and still had a twenty-nine-minute lead. But for the other places, a close race was unfolding. "The four canoes just behind the Chicagoans came into Little Falls in almost a dead heat yesterday, after a brisk lap on a cool day," Shave wrote.

One of those canoes held the Gunflint guides Clark and Zimmerman in second place. But on the river between Little Falls and St. Cloud, they had a rough time. "Only what is politely known as 'intestinal fortitude' kept Clark and Zimmerman from losing more precious minutes to their competitors for second place Saturday. ZIMMERMAN WAS SO ILL WHEN THEY LEFT LITTLE FALLS THAT IT WAS FEARED THE TEAM MIGHT HAVE TO GIVE UP. But he stuck it out while his valiant partner accepted the burden of strengthening his strokes to make up for Zimmerman's weakened condition." The pair hung on to their place, if barely, and found themselves in "A battle royal for second place" with the Canadians.

It was also announced that a special committee (a park board director, two reporters, and two sporting goods store owners) would rule on the legality of Oslund and Robinson's boat by the end of the race. Nonetheless, the grousing continued. "Stance 'All Wrong' But It's Still Good Enough to Win," read one headline, and the couple were repeatedly referred to as "tenderfeet" and "city slickers." The fact that the pair were from out of state, and from a big city—combined with their weird paddling style and their unusual canoe—marked them as outsiders and interlopers in what would have otherwise been a north woods, working-class race.

For their part, the Chicago team argued it was their paddling, not their canoe, that set them apart. And some suspected they were right: "derby officials are wondering if the 1941 Paul Bunyan canoe derby may not touch off a revolution in canoe racing technique," reported one article.

Letters poured in to the papers for and against the Chicago team.

A. T. Hansford, who sponsored another team in the race, wrote, "From watching them, I'd say that they take about 25 strokes to 45 for their competitors. If these boys can invent a better method of paddling and win the race MORE POWER TO THEM. If they win, they must be paid the winners' purse and receive the honors that go with it. . . . LET'S NOT SPOIL IT WITH ARGUMENTS ABOUT THE CHICAGO TEAM."

"If we were in tenth place," Oslund remarked, "I don't think there would be a protest." The Chicago team now had a thirty-minute lead and were comfortably in first place. But the race just behind them was still in play. On the lap from St. Cloud to Anoka, second-place Clark and Zimmerman capsized two minutes after the start. They lost eight minutes, and the Canadians Gaudry and Mathieson moved ahead of them.

And behind Clark and Zimmerman, the Heinemans were coming up fast. They won the lap from St. Cloud to Anoka, and by the next morning, with one lap to go, Clark and Zimmerman trailed the Canadians by three minutes—and led the Heinemans by three minutes.

"The third place struggle will be a bitter one when the teams hit the water at 1:00 P.M. today," wrote Shave.

The next day, nineteen remaining teams were ready to go. "Thirty-eight weary but determined canoeists were poised at Anoka today for the desperate lunge down the home stretch of the grueling 450-mile Aquatennial canoe derby," reported Shave. The brothers grabbed the lead: "the Heinemans swept down the river at a terrific pace, paddling at times over 55 strokes a minute to cover the final lap in 2:34:45, faster than any other team."

In Minneapolis, the bridges and shorelines were packed with an estimated 100,000 people watching the finish: "Large crowds lined the final route, being parked all along the riverbanks. . . . All bridges were thickly clustered." Once the canoes had reached the Third Avenue Bridge, they were portaged around the falls for the final sprint.

The Chicago team won that, and they won the whole derby with its $500 first prize (about $10,000 today). The special committee ruled that their craft "was a canoe and that it met specifications of the canoe race committee."

The Canadian team of Cleo Gaudry and Don Mathieson finished second and got $250. The Heinemans passed Clark and Zimmerman to snatch third place—and $125—by less than three minutes. In fifth were Mankato's Harvey Anderson, age forty-eight, and Augie Schueneman, thirty-two, followed by Harry and Bud Tibbetts.

"The Indian teams were bunched," wrote Shave, "taking sixth, seventh, eighth and ninth places. In ninth were the noted veteran paddlers, Jesse and Jim Tibbetts, who have been competing in canoe races for over 40 years."

There was talk of a grudge match between the Chicagoans and the other top teams, but it doesn't appear to have happened. Instead, Oslund and Robinson cut their losses—and their gains—and went home.

"It was a great race," Robinson said, "and I'm glad we won but I don't believe I'll be back for another."

He was planning to get married and didn't think he would have time.

THE VICTORY DERBY

1942

BY THE NEXT SUMMER, PEOPLE'S MINDS WERE NOT ON canoes or canoe racing. They were overseas with the troops fighting World War II, which the United States had formally entered in December 1941.

The papers carried less news about the Paul Bunyan Canoe Derby in the summer of 1942. The Aquatennial celebration, like everything else, took on a military tone. It was labeled the "On-To-Victory" Aquatennial, and the parade was dubbed the "Victory Parade," featuring jeeps and aircraft and model aircraft carriers. But the 1942 derby went ahead. It would be one of the closest and best races ever.

On Sunday morning, July 12, the racers once again gathered at Lake Bemidji near the statue of Paul Bunyan and Babe the Blue Ox. This year, the organizers offered $1,240 in prizes (about $24,000 now), including a "daily sprint" award of $10 for the racers who won the day's lap and $5 for second.

Of the thirty-six paddlers registered, twenty-three had raced in the derby before, including Walter and Orbid Heineman, ages thirty-three and thirty-one. The Heinemans, the paper said, were the team to watch: "Day after day they poured out energy hitting this fast stroke. The wonder was, and that wonder grew, how it could be done by a human being."

Given the 1941 controversy about what constitutes a canoe, the rules were stricter: this year canoes had to be canvas-covered, at least fifteen feet long, at least sixty pounds, and "of standard construction." Of the eighteen teams that registered, five were scratched on the morning of the race, "for attempting to enter the derby with canoes other than canvas-covered." Bill Little Wolf and his partner tried to find a canvas-covered canoe but couldn't, so they were out. Cleo Gaudry, the second-place winner in 1941, was also out because he couldn't get across the Canadian border in time for the start.

In the end, only nine teams set off from Bemidji on Sunday morning, including the Heinemans and Jesse and Leroy Goodin from Minneapolis, both of whom had raced in the derby before. Jesse Tibbetts and his brother Jim entered too, as did a certain Bill Evers of St. Paul, who was not Ojibwe but who was married to Jesse's daughter, Wanda. This was his first race, and before the start, he had never even been in a canoe.

At 9:00 AM, the paddlers set off across Lake Bemidji at one-minute intervals. The wind was fierce. One team got lost for three hours as high winds drove them off course on Cass Lake.

The Goodin brothers got to the Lake Winnibigoshish checkpoint first. Just behind them in second was a young racer whose name would become synonymous with canoeing in Minnesota. Karl Ketter, age twenty, and his partner Earl Couture, eighteen, both from north Minneapolis, finished forty-two seconds behind the Goodins. Another seven minutes behind them came the Heinemans, followed by Jesse and Jim Tibbetts, three minutes back. The first four teams were only twelve minutes apart.

The second day was the eighty-seven-mile lap to Grand Rapids. The racers woke at 3:30 AM for the sixteen-mile crossing of Lake Winnibigoshish. But the wind, blowing at thirty miles an hour, made the lake too dangerous, so the canoes were portaged around it.

The weather was cloudy and cool. This year, the derby had a University of Minnesota trainer, Lloyd Boyce, who helped the paddlers with cramps and gave them rubdowns. Yet the race still took its toll. On the second day, Couture got "severe stomach cramps," so he and Ketter slipped into third place. Jesse Tibbetts's "arm muscles went bad," though he and Jim held steady at fourth place.

The Goodins and the Heinemans "battled nip and tuck down the river and gave every indication that the event from now on would be a two-team race." At Jacobson, the Heinemans took the lap by one minute. In the next stage, "The Heinemans set a hot pace that brought them in nine minutes ahead of the Goodins." Yet their overall lead time was still just one minute and fifty-five seconds. The duel between the two teams was on.

"The number of entries in the Aquatennial canoe derby is the smallest since it started," wrote *Star Journal* columnist Charles Johnson, "but already the race gives promise of developing into one of the most exciting ever staged on the river."

The Goodins and Heinemans paddled neck and neck the whole way to Palisade. "Veteran observers at this lively town who have watched the Derbies since they started three years ago were thrilled at the brilliant racing Wednesday." The Heinemans won by half a canoe length.

Each day, the racers started at one-minute intervals in reverse order. That meant Jesse and Leroy Goodin started a minute ahead of the Heinemans, who worked all day to catch them, until they finally pulled ahead.

On the lap from Aitken to Brainerd, the Heinemans hit a rough patch, with Walter in a "weakened condition," according to the *Star Journal*. But he gutted it out: "Ill and weak from the intense heat yesterday, the gritty canoeist stayed in the race with his brother." The Heinemans still won the lap and gained a minute and twenty-five seconds on the Goodins.

In this grueling fashion, they extended their lead over the Goodins—a little over a minute a day. Before long, they were three minutes ahead. Then four. Then five.

Meanwhile, the newcomer Ketter hung on to third: "The tenacity with which Karl Ketter and Earl Couture, the youthful pair from Boutell's [Sporting Goods store] has been clinging to the leaders, has been the surprise of the derby."

Behind them, Jesse and Jim Tibbetts held on to fourth place.

On Saturday, the paddlers raced from Brainerd to St. Cloud. The weather turned bad, and the skies opened up. Eleven miles north of St. Cloud, just above the Sartell Dam—where the river is three-quarters of a mile wide—a violent storm swept in. Wind, rain, hail, thunder, and lightning pounded the river. The teams "headed for the west shore, all making cover and keeping on going in spite of high waves," wrote Ed Shave, the reporter who was following the racers in a motorboat. One canoe overturned, but the paddlers made it to land, emptied the boat, and continued. "We were lucky some of our boys in the Aquatennial Paul Bunyan canoe derby weren't drowned Saturday."

On the final lap from Anoka to Minneapolis, the Heinemans made a hard push. By then, they had muscled their way to a seven-minute, fifty-seven-second lead over the Goodin brothers, but they knew they couldn't let up, and neither could the Goodins. "So hard was the battle the final days," wrote Ed Shave, "and so furious the pace, the desperate Goodin boys, trying to grasp the lead, BROKE TWO PADDLES AND FINISHED WITH ONE."

As they pulled into Minneapolis, thousands of people lined the bridges and riverbanks to watch the finish. The paddlers stopped at the Third Avenue Bridge, then made the portage around St. Anthony Falls before finishing with a final sprint to the Franklin Avenue Bridge, which the Heinemans won.

Probably because of the Goodins' broken paddle, the Heinemans gained almost four minutes on the last day, leaving them with a final lead of nearly twelve minutes and clinching the $500 first prize. Their time was 62 hours, 54 minutes, and 14 seconds. It was "the closest finish in the history of the great event," wrote Ed Shave.

After the race, the Heinemans didn't hang around: "Walter Heineman, a brakeman on the road, said despite his winnings, he had to be back on the job." The brothers announced after the race that they would use their winnings to purchase war bonds to help fund the war effort.

The Goodin brothers finished second. During the race, Jesse had lost thirteen pounds, and Leroy had lost eight.

Karl Ketter and Earl Couture finished third, some two hours behind the Heinemans. Ketter said his partner was hungry the whole time and "even made me stop and bum a couple sandwiches at a farm on the third day."

In fourth place came Jesse and Jim Tibbetts, both in their late forties. Their wives, daughters, and "at least five Tibbetts grandchildren" were cheering for them at the finish.

"Those grand Indian veterans, Jesse and Jim Tibbetts of Deer River and Ball Club, surprised everyone by finishing fourth. It was not figured that the two old warriors could hold a pace for nine days to remain up with the leaders." This was especially noteworthy since Jesse didn't even train for the race. "'Old Jesse' admitted the only training they did was take a day off to rest before the start of the race," the *Morning Tribune* reported.

Even more surprising was his son-in-law, who had never been in a canoe before the start. "In fifth position was a new team of Bill Evers of Minneapolis and Russell Gamache of St. Paul," the *Morning Tribune* reported. "These lads were newcomers but they were aided by the Evers' father-in-law, Jesse Tibbetts. He piloted his son-in-law through many of the vast swamps and kept him from paddling into blind channels and getting off course at many lakes."

Compared to 1941, the race was congenial. There were no protests, and afterward Orbid Heineman, who was "shy and modest, took to worrying that he hadn't properly congratulated all the other contestants in the nine-canoe race."

Orbid's wife, who followed the race in a trailer and made sure the paddlers had a good breakfast every morning, summed up the spirit of the event. "Mrs. Orbid Heineman hit the nail on the head when she said, 'all 18 of the boys were wonderful, they believe in doing, not saying, and do they did.'"

THE SHORT COURSE

1943–1945

THE WAR CONTINUED. EVERYTHING ELSE WAS SECONDARY, including the derby.

In 1943, the race was changed to a four-lap course on the Chain of Lakes in Minneapolis, totaling forty-five miles. The race would follow the shorelines of Lake Calhoun, Lake of the Isles, and Cedar Lake. There was also "one 75-yard portage along the iron railed walk of Lake of the Isles." The purse was $547 in war bonds and stamps.

Thirty-seven teams entered the derby. Walter Heineman, LeRoy Goodin, and Richard Mattson—top finishers from previous derbies—all entered, each with a new partner. There were no Tibbettses on the list and few, if any, Native paddlers. Some of the new contestants included a state high school wrestling champion, later to become a professional wrestling legend, named Verne Gagne, who partnered with a certain Wayne Carlson. "Walter Heineman is one of the favorites," the *Sunday Tribune* reported. "However, he will be under a handicap as his partner, a fellow Crosby Minn. resident, Hugh Leach, has had very little previous canoeing experience."

On race day, only twenty-eight teams were at the start, and "A jam of spectators lined all the lakes." They day was hot. According to one account: "Thirst was a big problem in the derby. One contestant was seen drinking from Lake Calhoun to save time going to shore, but most teams had trainers who passed cool drinks and sandwiches to the canoes."

One racer, Don Biggins, had no legs. The judges offered to let him skip the portage, but he "refused a special ruling [and] showed his fighting spirit, not wanting to accept favors, and crawled over the portage by his hands."

Heineman and Leach won the race in 6 hours, 29 minutes, and 13 seconds. They received $150 in war bonds. Second was Leroy Goodin and his partner, and third were Richard Mattson with his brother Clarence.

Only seventeen teams finished. The list did not include Verne Gagne.

* * *

A few days before the 1944 Paul Bunyan Canoe Derby was scheduled to begin, a sad item appeared in the paper. Ed Eliason, forty years old and "one of the greatest outdoorsmen of the northland," had died. He was a fisherman in Grand Marais, and four years earlier he and his bother Ace had won the very first canoe derby. Eliason had been on his boat in the Grand Marais harbor when he either fainted or had a heart attack, fell overboard, and drowned.

With World War II going strong, there was plenty of tragedy unfolding around the world. Jesse Tibbetts's son, Jesse Jr., was killed in action on the English Channel in December. Young men were needed to fight the war, and many were already overseas, so the 1944 derby was reduced to a four-mile race and restricted to youth ages seventeen and under.

The race started on Sunday, July 30, at 2:00 PM, and was won by Ronny Anderson and Gene Coyer of Mankato. It was their first race. They were in second place until the last few hundred yards, when "the Mankato team put on the steam" and passed the leaders, finishing in thirty-four minutes and thirty-three seconds. Anderson's father was Harvey Anderson, who had finished third in the 1928 Diamond Jubilee race, and who had competed in both the 1940 and 1941 derbies, finishing fifth in 1941.

They next year, on July 22, 1945, the "wartime version of the Bemidji-to-Minneapolis race" was largely the same. Seventeen-year-olds Herbert Shoening and Lyle Johnson won in twenty-eight minutes and received gold medals. "Both are experienced canoe men and the pair finished a full minute ahead of" the second-place team.

THE RACE RETURNS

1946

BY THE SUMMER OF 1946, LIFE IN AMERICA WAS RETURNING to something like normal. Germany had surrendered more than a year earlier, and Japan the previous September. Minnesotans were ready to race, and the Paul Bunyan Canoe Derby was back. What's more, Warner Bros. had announced it was coming to town to film the derby with three thousand feet of technicolor film. The company was creating a "two-reel sports oddity" for one of its "Sports Shorts."

Getting the postwar race back on track, however, was a bit rough. Many who were eager to compete couldn't find canoes or sponsors. "Canoes are needed very badly for the Aquatennial's Paul Bunyan Canoe Derby from Bemidji to Minneapolis," wrote *Sunday Tribune* columnist Cedric Adams. "Several teams want to enter but can't locate a canoe." This included many "war veterans who have returned from long service overseas to find their canoes in poor repair."

Another problem was the lack of racers. Derby chair John Scheefe complained that "Either Minnesota's famed competitive spirit is lagging or our athletes are getting lazy." There was more money than ever at stake, with a total purse of $2,000 (almost $32,000 today) *and* a chance to be in the Warner Bros. film.

As the race got closer, more entries came in, including a pair of Ojibwe brothers from Ball Club named Jim and Bernie Smith.

Then an exciting headline ran the day before the race started. It said: "Tibbetts Teams Complete Picture for Canoe Derby." "The Tibbetts are paddling again," wrote Ed Shave. "No Paul Bunyan canoe race would be complete without one of the famous Indian family competing."

In fact, there would be three Tibbetts teams:

- Bob and Bud (also known as Marvin), who had been a top swimmer and baseball player in high school. Both had just been released from the navy. Bud had finished second in the 1940 derby, and they would be paddling the same canoe Ben Tibbetts and Bill Reynolds used to win the 1928 Diamond Jubilee race.
- Bill (the oldest racer, at fifty-six) and Tommy, who had been a "noted boxer" and who now worked as a traffic officer in Bemidji.
- Ray, paddling with his brother-in-law Bill Evers. Evers had never set foot in a canoe before the start of the 1942 derby, and had finished fifth overall.

The top of the field this year would be evenly divided between white and Native paddlers. Walter and Orbid Heineman, the former champions from Crosby-Ironton, were back—and the favorites. Also returning was longtime racer Harvey Anderson of Mankato with his partner Augie Schueneman, age thirty-eight. The two had trained on the Blue Earth River, paddling upstream against an eleven-mile-per-hour current, making one inch of progress per paddle stroke. Anderson, at fifty-three, had raced in 1928, 1940, and 1941.

The day before the race, on Tuesday, July 9, paddlers were weighed in and given medical exams, and their canoes were weighed in too. The Heinemans won the prerace, one-mile sprint, followed by Anderson and Schueneman, with a third-place tie between Bob and Bud Tibbetts and Ray Tibbetts and Bill Evers. That night the racers attended a banquet.

The next morning, a crowd of two thousand people—the largest so far—turned out on the shore of Lake Bemidji to watch the start. The parking lot had cars with license plates from twenty-eight states and Canada. Under a clear sky, with a "brisk" west wind, "Forty-four brawny paddlers dipped their blades in the glistening waters of Lake Bemidji today to start the first postwar Paul Bunyan Aquatennial canoe derby," read a story in the *Star Journal*. The twenty-one teams were released at the usual one-minute intervals. The Heinemans were the first to leave; Bob and Bud Tibbetts were eighteenth.

The water was rough. Five teams capsized in four-foot waves on Lake Bemidji and Cass Lake—one team tipped on both. Another team's canoe, while being towed, was "hurled against the propeller," putting several gashes in it. Then, nearing shore, it was damaged again, and one of the team's paddles was also broken. But they patched up all nine holes and kept going. (Teams that accepted a tow were given a five minute time penalty.)

With the Heinemans out front, Bob and Bud Tibbetts gave chase. "The famous Indian name of Tibbetts is flying high again in the canoeing world," wrote Ed Shave. "All day long the Indian paddlers passed teams on the rough waters of Lake Bemidji, down the river, and across Cass lake to the finish line of the first lap of the 450 mile grind."

Bob and Bud came in first with their storied canoe. Their time was one minute and thirty-six seconds off the record pace. The Heinemans were two minutes and fifteen seconds behind them.

The next morning, racers got up at 5:00 AM for the Lake Winnibigoshish crossing. But the wind was still high, and the lake was judged to be too dangerous. So officials called for trucks to haul the canoes from the west side of Winnibigoshish to the eastern outlet, where the racers would resume paddling.

That day the Heinemans, with their high stroke rate of "52 to 60 per minute," took the lead. "The 1942 victors hit a terrific pace, and broke all records from Winnibigoshish to the government dam" outside Grand Rapids. They beat the Goodin brothers' record on the lap by nearly an hour. This put them seven minutes ahead of Bob and Bud Tibbetts in second.

When the canoes reached Grand Rapids, there was a dinner followed by a series of ceremonial dances presented by "10 Indians from Deer River," according to the *Star Journal*.

The field narrowed. A team dropped out after one member learned his baby daughter was in a Minneapolis hospital. Another team quit when one of the paddlers had "[c]ramps from a piece of tainted meat." Tommy and Bill Tibbetts also dropped out, with no reason given. Soon there were only seventeen teams left.

That night, the Mankato team provided entertainment. "Clown of the race is Harvey Anderson. . . . One of the first teams to arrive here, he entertained onlookers with several musical selections on an ocarina."

On the third day, the Heinemans grew their lead to eleven minutes. The Mankato team was also gaining, moving up from fourth to third, but Bob and Bud Tibbetts fended them off. Ray Tibbetts and Bill Evers were in fourth, followed by Jim and Bernie Smith in fifth. Fully half of the top ten paddlers were Ojibwe.

The river was high and fast. On the next lap the first three teams were dueling all the way down. Bob and Bud Tibbetts started a minute ahead of the Heinemans. The leaders caught and passed them, but the Tibbettses stayed with them, and only conceded a minute.

When the Heinemans caught Anderson and Schueneman, they fought hard too. After seven-plus hours of paddling, the top three teams came into Palisade within three seconds of each other. Meanwhile, Jim and Bernie Smith moved into fourth, while Ray Tibbetts and Bill Evers slid to fifth.

The next stop was Orbid Heineman's hometown of Aitken. "When the canoeists arrived," Shave reported, "Mrs. Orbid Heineman, who is following . . . in a trailer, had lunch for all 17 teams." She had crewed for the brothers in 1941 and 1942 as well.

Twenty-five miles downstream was Walter's home of Crosby (the twin city of Ironton), where the town was planning to "sound all the whistles available 15 minutes before arrival to permit inhabitants to swarm the river. All business establishment will close to permit maximum attendance," Ed Shave reported. A local hotel owner served a light lunch to the paddlers, and they stopped for ten minutes to eat the sandwiches, even though they had just eaten upstream.

The race was a hard one—Bud Tibbetts would lose fourteen pounds by the end. But it was even harder for teams at the rear. "Blistered by sun, drenched by rains, arms weary and in some instances actually ill," wrote Jack Connor in the *Sunday Tribune*, "they continued on with no hope of getting in the big prize money or even improving their place in the race."

Even so, a duel was heating up between the two last-place teams. Bob Wilson, sixteen, and Butts Wilson, seventeen, were sprinting against Carl Fenske, seventeen, and George Stimmler, sixteen, when Bob tore some ligaments in his right arm. After the doctor advised him against continuing, tears welled up in his eyes. Fenske, for his part, had "a lower lip swollen to twice its normal size by the sun."

Still, there was camaraderie. Ray Horsch had been completely paralyzed by polio until two year earlier. Now he had more mobility, but he still had to cross the portages on crutches, so the other teams helped Horsch and his partner carry their canoe.

The Heineman brothers, fueled by sandwiches and the "tremendous ovation" at Aitken and Crosby, "staged their most furious paddling since the Paul Bunyan Aquatennial canoe derby started," reported the *Morning Tribune*. They broke the lap record set by the Chicago paddlers in 1941 and beat their own previous lap time by nearly an hour. In the fast water, five teams broke the 1941 record to Little Falls. Meanwhile, Jim and Bernie Smith finished third for the day and gained four minutes on the Mankato duo.

On Friday, July 2, as they raced the last lap into Minneapolis, the Heinemans extended their lead. They reached the city at 2:00 PM, where 100,000 spectators were expected to watch the finish. "The paddling Heinemans," wrote Ed Shave, "engraved their names Friday in lasting letter on the walls of Minnesota's hall of canoe racing fame."

They also won the sprint to the Franklin Avenue Bridge. Their total time of 58 hours, 17 minutes, and 51 seconds beat the 1941 record by four and a half hours and won them the $500 first prize. Bob and Bud Tibbetts came in second ($300); Harvey Anderson and Augie Schueneman third ($200); Jim and Bernie Smith fourth ($100); and Ray Tibbetts and Bill Evers fifth ($80).

Sixteen of the twenty-one teams that started made it to Minneapolis. The last-place teenagers Fenske and Stimmler finished twenty-two hours behind the leaders—a full three days of paddling.

Boney Selinsky, who finished second to last, summed up the general sentiment. "If I had known what I know now I wouldn't get in this thing for $2,000," he told reporter Jack Connor, who then added: "Now he's talking about entering the race next year."

TIBBITTS'S TRIUMPH

1947

ON MAY 25, 1947, AN ARTICLE APPEARED IN THE *MINNEAPOLIS Sunday Tribune* with the headline, "One-time Wrestler, Son in Canoe Derby." The story was about Billy Smith Sr., a former professional wrestler, and his son, Billy Smith Jr., who were planning to compete in the Paul Bunyan Aquatennial Canoe Derby. The father weighed 202 pounds. "He is a bricklayer by trade, but has wrestled on professional cards here and did a wartime USO tour with Strangler Smith, who he wrestled 27 times." They had been training on the Mississippi River between the Camden Bridge and Anoka. The article featured a photo of the younger Smith, who weighed 138 pounds, feeling his father's muscular arm.

Billy Smith Sr. and Jr. training for the 1947 derby. *Photo courtesy of Timothy Atchley*

"The first race was my dad's idea," says Smith, now ninety-three. "He was strictly out for self-promotion. He was a professional wrestler and everything was hype. Anything for attention was good. You know: 'I don't care what you say about me. Just spell my name, right.' That kind of stuff. I had just turned sixteen, so I just went along for the ride."

This year, there was again strong interest from Ojibwe racers, with at least six teams entering the derby. "This looms as a big year for the paddling Chippewas in the Paul Bunyan race," wrote Ed Shave. "At least, that's the surging hope and ambition of genial Jess Tibbetts who has been identified with all the Aquatennial canoe classics, first as a competitor, and later as a coach of the colorful Indian duets. Last year Indian teams placed second, fourth and fifth."

Not since the 1928 Diamond Jubilee race had an Ojibwe team won. This year, Tibbetts hoped to change that. His son Ray Tibbetts and son-in-law Bill Evers (who was not Ojibwe) were racing together. The two had paddled together in 1942 and 1946 and had finished fifth both times. If one of Jesse Tibbetts's teams won, it would be the culmination of a lifetime's work of canoeing, racing, and coaching.

But Tibbetts and Evers's race was in real doubt. Shortly before the 1947 derby, Ray had been in a car accident and suffered "a severely lacerated left wrist, the tendons being severed," Ed Shave reported on May 30. "Physicians are dubious that he can paddle in time for the July 9th start."

Ray wasn't sure he could race either, but in the end he decided he would try. The two didn't start training until two weeks before the derby.

On Tuesday, July 8, at the Bemidji Water Carnival, there was a sprint race, which Orbid and Walter Heineman, two-time derby champions, won. They were followed by Karl Ketter and a new kid named Irwin "Buzzy" Peterson.

Jim and Bernie Smith were also in the mix. "The Smith brothers," wrote Ed Shave, "Jim and Bernie, fifth-place finishers a year ago, appear in much better condition and will be stroking a vastly improved canoe." Shave also reported that "Crafty Jess Tibbetts has painstakingly rebuilt the No. 33 canoe in which Bob and Bud Tibbetts finished second last year. It then weighed 110 pounds—now it is a streamlined 68." This was the same boat that Ben Tibbetts had loved, lost, and regained—and in which he had won the five-hundred-mile 1928 Diamond Jubilee canoe race.

On Wednesday morning, all sixty-four paddlers gathered at Lake Bemidji. Governor Luther Youngdahl was on hand to start the race. Harvey Anderson of Mankato, ever the jokester, "presented the governor with a red and white fishing plug 12 inches long so he 'could catch bigger fish.'"

At 9:00 AM, Youngdahl fired the starting gun, and the racers set off in pairs at one-minute intervals. This year, the "Crosby-Ironton speedsters" wouldn't have it so easy: Ray Tibbetts and Bill Evers finished the lap one minute ahead of the champs.

At 3:30 AM the next day, the teams were up. Breakfast was at 4:00 AM, and at 5:00 AM they were ready to cross Lake Winnibigoshish, for only the second time in the derby's history. The canoes were

Governor Luther Youngdahl fires the shot to start the 1947 derby. The statue of Paul Bunyan and a Ferris wheel can be seen on the horizon. Billy Smith Sr. and Jr. wait for the gun. *MNHS*

escorted by motorboats, and about halfway across, a south wind started kicking up whitecaps. Bill Wakefield and Jimmy Wilson had to be assisted when their canoe took on too much water. They were penalized, but kept going.

By the end of the day, four teams had dropped out, including the Heinemans, after Walter "succumbed to cramps" and "was near collapse" on the way across Winnibigoshish. The champs were done. "On their arrival," reported Jack Connor in the *Star*, "they loaded up their car and headed back for Crosby."

This left Tibbetts and Evers with a fourteen-minute lead, ahead of Karl Ketter and Buzzy Peterson, followed by Ed King and Dick Peck in third, and Jim and Bernie Smith in fourth.

Meanwhile, back in the middle of the pack, young Billy Smith Jr. was in rough shape. "A blister that completely covered the palms of his hands made Thursday's jaunt misery for 16-year-old Billy Smith Jr. . . . The elder Smith brought the boy to a Grand Rapids physician for treatment before the start of today's lap."

Today Smith recalls it differently. "My dad would hide me from the doctors," he says, "because if they would have found out how bad my hands were, they would pull me out of the race, and there goes his chance to be a big shot. He was a very egotistical guy, always looking out for himself."

Up front, Tibbetts and Evers fended off Ketter and Peterson. On the lap from Grand Rapids to Jacobson, they were only fourteen minutes ahead. On the next leg, the north Minneapolis boys cut the lead to eleven minutes.

On the fourth day, at the town of Palisade, Ray Tibbetts was rushed to the hospital because the blisters on his hand were infected. But the next morning, he was back in full force. "With his raw, swollen, infected hands powdered with disinfectant, wrapped in gauze and bandaged, Ray Tibbetts and his wiry little brother-in-law Bill Evers . . . waged a gritty duel Sunday and gained eight precious minutes over Karl Ketter and Irwin C. Peterson."

Jim and Bernie Smith, in fourth place, also almost moved up, gaining six minutes on the team in front of them. But as the stakes rose, so did the tension. "Tempers flared, nerves exploded and the canoe derby experienced one of its most tempestuous days in its history," reported Shave.

Some teams claimed others took short cuts though the winding river sections. Ketter and Peterson lodged a protest against Evers and Tibbetts for altering their boat.

"Saturday night astute old Jesse Tibbetts," wrote Shave, "narrowed [the beam of] canoe No. 30 and as a result it apparently cut the river waters much better than previously."

Ketter argued that no change should be made to the canoe after the start of the race, but the judges denied the protest.

Meanwhile, the paddlers were suffering a variety of ailments: "inflamed cords" in the back, an inflamed thumb, bursitis in the shoulder, stomach cramps, and illness. At one point, the partner of polio survivor Ray Horsch was so sick he had to lie in the bottom of the canoe for three hours while Horsch—a powerful paddler—rowed by himself. Alone, he boosted their team's position from nineteenth to thirteenth, passing Billy Smith Jr. and his dad along the way.

"My dad was not a very good canoer," says Smith today. "There was no technique. He'd power his way through and the canoe would be jumping up and down and bouncing around. The good news is that, the way the race goes is the slowest teams always start first. So if you're a slow team, every day you get to see the fast guys go by, which is a good time to learn what really good canoers are. And at that time those were the Indians from up around Ball Club, Minnesota. They were the canoe builders. When the Indians went by, they actually glided by rather than bounced by."

Glide by they did. And if Tibbetts and Evers glided to victory, it would be a significant one. It would be "the first [derby] ever won by a team that included one Indian—Ray Tibbetts," wrote Jack Connor in the *Star*, anticipating the finish. "The performance of Ray, handicapped by blisters, and his partner Bill Evers, is a tribute to the astute coaching of Jesse Tibbetts, Bemidji Indian."

After Ketter and Peterson's protest was denied, between Brainerd and Little Falls they tried to take first place the hard way. "By sheer grit and power," reported Ed Shave, leaning into stereotypes, "they attempted to narrow the gap between themselves and the first place Chippewa Indians, Ray Tibbetts and Bill Evers. But it was not so written in the book. The two canoes raced bow to bow most of the way, but in a thrilling finish the braves gained another precious minute and six seconds."

When the paddlers arrived in Little Falls, Ketter and Peterson proposed a one-mile grudge match against Tibbetts and Evers on Lake Calhoun after the derby was over. The teams would exchange canoes. Evers and Tibbetts, who had a seventeen-minute overall lead, agreed. Ketter's sponsor, Corrie's Sporting Goods, put up a $50 prize for first place and a $25 prize for second.

On the leg from St. Cloud to Anoka, Ketter and Peterson "made another desperate drive . . . but were unable to pick up more than two minutes" on Evers and Tibbetts.

Then on Friday afternoon, July 18, the racers swept into Minneapolis, where an estimated ten thousand people had gathered to watch the finish. Attendance may have been down from the early derby crowds of 100,000 spectators. Or estimates may have been getting more precise. Either way, a lot of people stood watching as Jim and Bernie Smith came in first, winning the lap. After all the other teams had arrived, they portaged around the falls for the final sprint.

Evers and Tibbetts won that too, along with the $50 prize money on top of the $500 for first place in the derby. Their time was 58 hours, 17 minutes, and 51 seconds—thirteen minutes and ten seconds ahead of Karl Ketter and Buzzy Peterson.

Ed Shave wrote, "Stoic old Jesse Tibbetts of the Chippewa clan Friday evening did a dance on the banks of the Mississippi which reminds me of a highland fling which I witnessed years ago on the banks of Scotland's Loch Lomond. He was rightly cutting capers because his broad-shouldered son Ray, and son-in-law Bill Evers, had just captured the 1947 Paul Bunyan Aquatennial Canoe Derby championship in a canoe the crafty hands of old Jesse had constructed." Or more precisely, a canoe he had reconstructed, and which had previously won the Diamond Jubilee race in 1928.

Spectators on a Minneapolis bridge, about 1947. *MNHS*

Crowds watch the final sprint race in 1947 from the west bank of the Mississippi, above the Franklin Avenue Bridge. *MNHS*

But that wasn't the only reason Jesse Tibbetts was dancing: he had coached five of the top ten teams in the derby.

Billy Smith Jr. and his dad finished in thirteenth place. Now that the younger Smith had seen what good paddlers could do, he was sure he could do better.

Blackie Jarnig, who had also raced in 1940, finished in twenty-first place. Jarnig had served four years in World War II as a paratrooper and glider trooper in Belgium, Holland, and Germany. He had been badly injured in a glider accident, then spent fourteen months in military hospitals. Soon after he was released from the hospital, he signed up for the derby. A reporter asked why.

"Well," he said, "the canoe derby gets in your blood I guess."

* * *

At 3:00 PM the next Sunday, the top two teams met at the south end of Lake Calhoun for their grudge match—each in the other team's canoe. Another crowd estimated at ten thousand people gathered to watch.

The gun went off. There were strong winds, so Tibbetts and Evers had trouble managing their boat, which rode high in the water and caught the wind. They were forced to go far to the right, then tack back into the wind. Ketter and Peterson, on the other hand, cut straight across the lake, and finished fifty-eight seconds ahead of the champions.

Because of the winds, the race didn't settle the debate. "As a result," wrote Ed Shave, "arguments over what might have happened in the 450-mile race will continue from here on."

Two things, however, were clear. First: Jesse Tibbetts's storied canoe was something special. Jack Connor reported that Tibbetts "plans to construct several racing models to enter a group of Indian teams in the 1948 derby." Second: Tibbetts and Evers were officially "the champion long distance canoeists of the United States." Governor Luther Youngdahl issued a challenge to all other governors to send a team who could beat them.

Enthusiasm for the derby was at an all-time high. Next year, it seemed, it would be bigger and better.

DANCING ON THE WATER

1948

THE FOLLOWING YEAR, BILLY SMITH JR. DECIDED NOT TO RACE again. Instead he agreed to drive and provide support for two young paddlers from his neighborhood in north Minneapolis. Eugene Jensen and Tom Estes were nineteen and twenty-one years old. They were part of a group that trained on the Mississippi River above St. Anthony Falls. Jensen was a laborer. Estes was an assembly worker.

The 1948 race would be the sixth Paul Bunyan Aquatennial Canoe Derby. "There are more well-conditioned duos in the race than ever before," reported Ed Shave. "Many of the teams have been in hard training for several weeks." Hopes were high for the Ojibwe contingent. "More Indian teams than ever before are planning to enter. Bemidji's Jesse Tibbetts, 'guardian angel' of the Indian canoe teams in past years, has five pairs now ready to enter and three more seriously considering it."

The previous year's champions, Ray Tibbetts and Bill Evers, were planning to enter. "Ray has trimmed down from 195 pounds to 172 through wood cutting all winter. And Bill, who started last year's race at 164 and ended it at 149, now weights 153." They would be paddling a new boat, which was a homemade canoe modeled on the Peterborough, "a trim, slim, narrow beamed craft with speed in every line." Jim and Bernie Smith, who placed fourth in 1947, were back with their own canoe they'd built, as were Bob and Bud Tibbetts, who had placed second in 1946.

Jesse Tibbetts was also trying to recruit teams from the Red Lake and Nett Lake Ojibwe reservations, and was even thinking of entering himself with his brother Jim, who was "59 years young." The two had finished fourth in the 1942 derby.

The overall purse was $2,800, with $1,000 for first place (just over $12,700 in today's dollars), $500 for second, $300 for third, and so on. There were also prizes—mostly Scott-Atwater outboard motors—for winning some of the daily laps.

By the time the race started, thirty teams had registered, including a twenty-two-year-old Harlow Thompson and his cousin Gordon Kossow.

"My uncle was in it," said Thompson in a 2024 interview, at age ninety-nine, "and I had just got out of the service. So I went and watched in 1947, and I thought, 'That looks sort of fun. Maybe I should try it.'"

On Tuesday, July 14, there was a one-mile sprint the night before the derby's start. Ray Tibbetts and Bill Evers "served notice" by winning.

The next morning the teams gathered again along the shore of Lake Bemidji. A strong east wind blew, while several safety boats patrolled the lakes looking for capsized canoes.

The race didn't start as expected. Tibbetts and Evers were in the lead, but just as they came into Wolf Lake—the first lake after Lake Bemidji—they hit a sharp rock running some rapids, which ripped four feet of canvas off the canoe. The tear proved impossible to repair. The team was out. "Both were extremely despondent," Jack Connor reported.

Karl Ketter and Buzzy Peterson made it further, but on Cass Lake their new V-bottom canoe, which they'd just gotten on Monday and hadn't even paddled until the sprint, couldn't ride the big waves. After swamping three times, they too dropped out.

With the two top contenders gone, the field was wide open.

Bud and Bob Tibbetts won the first lap, setting a new record time. Jim and Bernie Smith came in second, and Deer River miners

King and Peck were third, while Kossow and Thompson were fifth. By the end of the first day, even with Tibbetts and Evers out, four of the top eight teams were Ojibwe paddlers. Yet there was another team waiting for their chance.

"The surprise team of the race is the No. 13 duet of Eugene Jensen and Tom Estes," wrote Ed Shave. "These newcomers, paddling a new, streamlined Peterborough canoe, finished in fourth place." The boys from north Minneapolis didn't know the river. So they had to stay in the main channel, while others were able to cut through certain places. Soon three teams got ahead of them.

The next day, the racers were up at 5:00 AM for the Lake Winnibigoshish crossing. But it was too windy and dangerous, so organizers decided to truck the canoes around the lake. Bob Tibbetts was on top of one of the trucks when he slipped, tried to jump off backward, caught his heel on a rope, and landed on his head and left shoulder. A doctor who was vacationing in the area taped up the shoulder.

Tibbetts started the day trying to paddle. He went "over half the distance," but the pain was too much, so he and Bud Tibbetts dropped out. Bob was taken to the hospital at Deer River, where an X-ray showed his shoulder was dislocated.

The field opened wider. Estes and Jensen passed Jim and Bernie Smith, then reeled in third-place King and Peck. "After the Minneapolis youths had caught the Deer River canoe," wrote Ed Shave, "they matched stroke for stroke down the Mississippi, with Jensen and Estes finally pulling ahead near the finish."

"Furious paddling allowed Eugene Jensen and Tom Estes to jump from third to first place," reported Jack Connor. They were in canoe number thirteen, but they told Connor they didn't believe in superstitions. And anyway, it seemed like luck was on their side.

Billy Smith, who was driving for Estes and Jensen, stopped at bridges to lower water and food on a rope. He met them with supplies at the end of the day. And every day, while he watched the other teams go by, there was one canoe that caught his eye: Jim and Bernie Smith's.

"While I was driving for Estes and Jensen," Smith says, "I noticed that Jim and Bernie Smith were literally dancing on the waves, like a surfer going on top of the water. And I noticed the way Jim and Bernie Smith paddled, with quick strokes. I watched them paddle by me every day. It was poetry in motion to watch that boat go."

But it wasn't just their paddling that was beautiful to watch. It was also their boat.

"Jim and Bernie Smith were excellent canoe builders. They said they could go into the woods and come out seven days later with the canoe.... I saw their canoe and I admired it very much. It was a design with a low bow. It really had some beautiful lines to it. Once you got up to a certain speed it could ride that speed without rocking if you were a smooth paddler. So it was strictly me falling in love with that canoe."

Estes and Jensen showed no sign of slowing down. Their lead grew to twelve minutes. But at Aitken, King and Peck cut that back to seven and a half minutes. Jensen was interviewed there by the *Sunday Tribune*. "'We watched the Derby last year and figured we might have had a one chance in 10 of winning,' said Jensen, munching an orange which is the team's daily noon diet on the river. 'This year we figure our chances at about one to five. . . . I guess we're just lucky some of those other good teams are out. But, of course, we're not done either and anything can happen between here and Minneapolis.'"

The next day, Estes and Jensen pushed their lead back up to sixteen minutes. The weather was cool, but the river was low. They had to shorten their strokes in the shallow water, and the paddles occasionally got stuck in the mud.

Bernie Smith was having more trouble with a "wrenched shoulder." He and Jim were still over an hour ahead of fifth place, so if they held on, fourth place was all theirs. Their wives, Theresa and Virginia Smith, were driving along with the paddlers. The *Star* reported, "they're the race's most avid fans. Wherever a road leads down to the river, they're there to cheer their teams on and nervously watch for signs of fatigue. They're as interested when the total elapsed times are figured each evening as any of the paddlers themselves."

Second-place King and Peck kept pushing the leaders. They won the lap to Brainerd (along with two Scott-Atwater outboard motors), carving a minute off Estes and Jensen's lead. The first three canoes finished within a minute of each other, in "one of the closest heats in the six-year history of the canoe race."

The paddlers suffered. "Many had lips so blistered by the sun, they could talk only with difficulty. Others were victims of cramp nausea and cramps," Shave reported.

The next lap, from Brainerd to Little Falls, was equally hard fought. The first four teams were separated by just a minute and twenty-six seconds. "For three consecutive days [King and Peck] have endeavored to gain on the leaders, but have only been able to

Tom Estes and Gene Jensen arriving at Nicollet Island, just above the Falls of St. Anthony, July 1948. Canoes were trucked around the falls for the final sprint race. *Minneapolis Morning Tribune, July 22, 1948*

whittle the margin from 19 minutes to 15 and they are rapidly running out of laps," wrote Ed Shave in the *Morning Tribune*. "The boys from north Minneapolis . . . have been able to meet every challenge."

As the racers went from Little Falls to St. Cloud, Bernie Smith was back to form. "The Smith Brothers . . . went all out Wednesday in a supreme effort to pick up on the leaders . . . but their efforts went for naught even though they beat last year's time by nearly nine minutes." The two canoes "came highballing into the finish line with the leaders being first by a narrow margin of only five seconds. It was one of the closest laps ever staged in the history of the race."

The push from the Smith brothers had boosted Estes and Jensen's lead over King and Peck back to nineteen minutes. Barring catastrophe, they had it in the bag.

As the teams raced down the final stretch into Minneapolis, an estimated twenty thousand people gathered to watch the finish. King and Peck won the final lap (and two more outboards), but Estes and Jensen won the derby and the $1,000 prize. "Two years of planning and training paid off," wrote Ed Shave.

"We'll be in again next year," said Jensen. He told reporters that they "actually enjoyed" the race, and that if someone "would put up another G-note," they'd do it again next week.

In fourth place were Jim and Bernie Smith, ages forty-nine and forty-six. They took home $150—just under $2,000 in today's dollars. And they were about to pick up a little more: After the race, seventeen-year-old Bill Smith Jr. approached Jim and Bernie about their boat. "When we got to Minneapolis," Smith says, "I had them drop over to the house. I said 'Bring the canoe. I'd like to buy it.' I think it was $100 [about $1,300 today], which I didn't have at the time. So I traded them a couple of my best guns as collateral, and said I'll send you $10 a month until the canoe is paid up. So for ten months, I sent them the payments. Jesse Tibbetts was the holder of the guns. And when I got it paid in full, he had the guns shipped back to me."

THE CANOE THAT CHANGED EVERYTHING

1949

BILL SMITH, NOW EIGHTEEN, SET HIS SIGHTS ON THE 1949 Paul Bunyan Canoe Derby. He found a partner, a speed skater in his thirties named Bob Bergstrom. Together, they took Smith's new canoe down to the Mississippi River. "We tipped over all the time," Smith says. "Just all the time. If you'd miss a signal and you switched wrong and you both end up on the same side, forget about it: you're tipping over. So we'd just tip over, tip over, tip over, until we finally got the hang of it. I guess Bob liked swimming because he decided to go in with me."

Bill was also good friends with another Bob who lived in Minneapolis: Robert Vaughn, a seventeen-year-old who would grow up to be an actor (playing, among many other roles, Napoleon Solo in the 1960s TV show *The Man From U.N.C.L.E.*). Vaughn also tried to paddle Jim and Bernie Smith's canoe, but he couldn't keep it upright either. "Bob did try, and we had fun watching him," Smith recalls. "He kept tipping over! But he had absolutely no interest in canoe racing. He was an actor."

In a way, Smith says, the canoe almost seemed like it was designed for tipping. "It kind of flared at the top," he recalls, "around the gunnels, so you would fall out before the boat would tip. But once you both got your paddles in the water, that would steady it, and once you got going it wasn't as tippy." Smith and Bergstrom practiced by traveling to Brainerd and paddling 140 miles down to Minneapolis, which Smith called "kind of a milk run."

On July 4 there was a series of preliminary races, including one from Fort Ripley to Minneapolis. The paddlers started at intervals of two minutes, so it was hard to tell where everyone finished. Tom Estes and Gene Jensen were in the race too. "They were paddling a V-bottom boat," says Smith. "One time they got hung up on some shallows. And I remember the cussing and swearing and them pushing off this shelf. And we said 'Too bad, too bad!' But once they got out of there, towards the finish line, it was the deep water. And V-bottoms do okay in deep water, so they caught up to us."

Just how close Smith and Bergstrom had come to beating them wasn't clear until that evening. "Estes and Jensen already had a reputation for being, by far away, the top guys in the canoe industry," says Smith. "And at the dinner afterwards they announced that we were only twenty-nine seconds behind them. I remember

Bob Bergstrom and Billy Smith Jr., paddling Jim and Bernie Smith's famous canoe in the 1949 qualifying race. *Photo courtesy the author*

all the guys at the table actually sucked in their breath. It was very audible. No one had ever come that close to beating them. And now here's little Billy Smith Jr. and Bob Bergstrom giving them a run for the money. That would have been the first time they'd ever gotten beaten in any race. And that scared them."

After such a close call, Estes and Jensen began investigating the new threat. "We'd practice a lot between Anoka and Minneapolis, and after we came close to beating them, they'd wait for us, up just around what would be 694. They'd wait behind one of the islands, watch us go by, them come in behind and compare. That's the only way they had of knowing who had a faster boat. And they realized that we had the faster boat, and that the V-bottom was not the way to go."

It was too late for them to change: Estes and Jensen had made a V-bottom, which plows through the water, for the 1949 race. So that's what they were going to race in. Fortunately, they were in excellent condition: Jensen had rigged up a paddle attached to a pulley system in his garage with a greased slide, and they trained all winter. Going into the derby, he and Estes would be the fittest paddlers on the water.

The stakes were high: the 1949 race was the biggest and best derby yet. Fifty teams entered the race, competing for slices of the $10,000 pie—just over $130,000 in today's dollars. The first-place prize was $2,000 ($26,000), and much of the money came from the Minnesota and Ontario ("M and O") Paper Company, which is why the 1949 race was renamed the Mando-Aquatennial Canoe Derby.

The 1949 derby would also see the first woman racing since Dorothy Messing in 1940. Grace Sunde, a forty-three-year-old mother of twelve (nine living) and a grandmother, was signed up.

The race would be fast. Three weeks of heavy rain had raised the water levels by twelve inches. The river was swollen, and the back channels were flooded and confusing.

On the morning of Friday, July 15, forty-eight canoes lined up at the start. Approximately three thousand people watched from shore, from docks, and from boats on Lake Bemidji. A few had even chartered seaplanes.

At 9:00 AM, Governor Youngdahl raised the starting gun and pulled the trigger. Nothing happened. "The tense contestants in the 450-mile derby laughed as Youngdahl waved the gun with a flourish, but couldn't get it to fire," reported Barbara Flanagan in the *Minneapolis Morning Tribune*. On his second try, it made enough noise to start the first wave across the lake, and Youngdahl yelled, "Go ahead!"

Grace Sunde, in an aluminum canoe, got the biggest cheer as she and her partner, Bernard Monson, "paddled briskly" out into Lake Bemidji.

In the high water, the race was on. On the first day, the top four teams finished within four minutes of each other. First across the line were Estes and Jensen. Second was a young team from Bemidji, Eric Hughes and Harold Westby, followed by Buzzy Peterson and his brother Floyd. This was the race in which Bill Smith broke two paddles before he and Bergstrom even crossed the first lake, after which Jim and Bernie Smith threw him a spare. With that paddle in hand, the two surprised themselves by finishing in seventh on the first lap, just behind the 1947 champions Ray Tibbetts and Bill Evers. Jim and Bernie Smith were down in twelfth.

Sunde and Monson finished the first lap in forty-third place. This was deemed newsworthy because Grace was forty-three years old, and her canoe was number forty-three. She told reporters: "It's not as tough as cutting wood."

On day two, Saturday, the paddlers set off at 5:00 AM across Lake Winnibigoshish, on the eighty-seven-mile lap to Grand Rapids. For only the third time in race history, they crossed the lake rather than being trucked around it. "Every resorter on that lake was on hand with boats to patrol the course," reported the *Sunday Tribune*. Several boats capsized, but rescuers were nearby. Bill Smith and Bob Bergstrom swamped and were rescued by Jesse Tibbetts—a detail that was never reported. Other teams were not so lucky: in addition to the six teams that dropped out Friday, nine more left the race after the second day. Ray Tibbetts and Bill Evers both became "very ill" and were taken to a physician, while Bob Tibbetts and Pat Murphy also got sick and dropped out.

Gerard Du Four and Gene Le May, a team from Quebec, finished in fourth place on the first day of the 1949 derby. *MNHS*

One of the casualties was Dick Peck and his nephew Harlow Thompson.

"We had bad luck on big Winni," Thompson recalled seventy-five years later. "We tipped over in the middle of the lake, and they never got us for two or three hours. They had safety boats, but not enough. So we just dropped out."

Asked whether being in the water that long wasn't dangerous, Thompson responded, "We was pretty young. It didn't bother us."

Along the rivers, crowds gathered at every dam and bridge. Most of the time this was great for morale. But Bill Smith recalls a crowd that didn't cheer quite so loudly. "One time," says Smith, "Bob had to urinate, and I steadied the canoe while he decided to stand. We came around a bend in full view of a bridge of cheering Crosby-Ironton fans. The surprised crowd was hushed and I could feel our canoe shake as Bob struggled to regain his balance and composure, and I struggled to keep us upright. It was humorous to me, but for Bob not so much."

At the front of the field, Estes and Jensen increased their lead every day. Behind them were Buzzy and Floyd Peterson, followed by Eric Hughes and Harold Westby, both high-level college athletes. But Smith and Bergstrom were right on their tails. "We were competing against guys who were in very good condition," says Smith. "And here we were, little Billy Smith Jr. and Bob Bergstrom, a speed skater. And because of our technique, we managed to stay up with the big guys."

At Aitken, Smith and Bergstrom were one of only three teams who made the lap in less than nine hours. "Most of the fireworks were furnished by Bergstrom and Smith as they advanced from seventh position to fourth," wrote Ed Shave. "Smith is in his second race and is paddling to win in order that he may continue this fall at the University of Minnesota. The game little fellow has a bad shoulder and severely blistered hands which necessitated the attendance of a physician, but the word 'quit' is not in his vocabulary."

Now Hughes and Westby were just ahead of them. "We were racing for third," says Smith. "We tipped over and spent more time swimming than we did canoeing, but we were still right behind them. We were faster, but you had to have the canoe in the water. The guys ahead of us paddled a Peterborough, and there was no competition between the Peterborough and our design from Jim and Bernie Smith. Not even close."

Jim and Bernie Smith, however, were not faring well. They'd moved up to seventh place, but then decided to drop out while they were still close to home. Somewhere around Aitken, Smith saw them sitting on the shore with some friends. "We chatted for a bit and that's when I found out that they'd decided to not continue," Smith recalls. "They had to make a decision, and they decided the money wasn't there for them. If they continued, all of a sudden they're down in Minneapolis, which was not Indian friendly, if we're being honest about it."

So the Smith brothers stayed in Indian country, while Bill paddled on in their former canoe. Now in fourth place, Smith and Bergstrom made a push. "Billy Smith and Bob Bergstrom of Minneapolis gave notice Tuesday that they intend to move up fast on the field in the 450-mile Mando-Aquatennial Canoe Derby," wrote Ed Shave. "These boys, paddling canoe No. 3., picked up 18 minutes and 15 seconds on the third place team of Eric Hughes and Harold Westby. . . . That feat, along with the 13 minutes they gained Monday, leaves them only 36 minutes behind the Bemidji pair. Their desperate paddling in the last two days has been the feature of this grueling event."

Up front, Estes and Jensen were running away. "We never stop to rest or eat," Jensen told the *Star*. "We paddle hard the first two hours or so every day to pass all the other canoes, then we lag off and just hold a steady pace of 44 strokes a minute." They were thirty-two minutes ahead of second place, and ten hours ahead of last-place Grace Sunde, who was "given a great ovation by her family" when she and Monson passed her home of Riverton.

The first two teams were paddling canoes they'd made themselves. Buzzy and Floyd Peterson had a canoe made of maple and plywood. Estes and Jensen had a tan, eighteen-foot plywood boat with a deep V-bottom and a thirty-inch beam.

Between Little Falls and Brainerd, Smith and Bergstrom made

another push. "Bob Bergstrom and Billy Smith Jr. of Minneapolis were desperately trying to edge into the third place spot now held by Eric Hughes of Bemidji and Harold Westby of Effie. Bergstrom and Smith were only 36 minutes and three seconds behind Hughes and Westby after pressuring them all the way."

They had gained half an hour in the last two days. But now. Hughes and Westby were putting up a fight. "The two canoes raced bow to bow all the way from Brainerd to Little Falls and almost ended in a dead heat. Smith and Bergstrom were able to gain only three seconds."

By now, there was only one Ojibwe team left in the race, Gilbert Jordan and Jim Hunt, in ninth place. And the derby's sole female paddler, Grace Sunde, had pulled a muscle in her shoulder when a wind gust caught the canoe, but she and her partner still were determined to finish. "I just don't want them to say that a woman couldn't make it," she said.

The next lap, from Little Falls to St. Cloud, saw Smith and Bergstrom's luck turn south: facing a strong headwind, they capsized three times, adding six minutes to the gap between them and third place. This gulf would prove unbridgeable over the two days remaining.

On Friday afternoon, twenty-six canoes raced into Minneapolis. An estimated twenty thousand people lined the bridges and shorelines. Estes and Jensen arrived first. After the paddlers had all landed, they were trucked around St. Anthony Falls for the final sprint. Only this year, the sprint would go all the way to the Ford Parkway Bridge, some five miles downstream.

Estes and Jensen won that too.

Their overall time for the derby was 56 hours, 53 minutes, and 4 seconds. This was forty-four minutes ahead of second-place Buzzy and Floyd Peterson, and it beat Ray Tibbetts and Bill Evers's 1947 record by more than five hours.

Grace Sunde and her partner finished last. But she did prove that a woman, a mother, and a grandmother could do the derby.

After the race, most teams were convinced that Estes and

Jensen's advantage was their V-bottom boat. Many announced they'd be back next year with the same. "We'll be back with one of those V bottom waters slicers," said a racer from Michigan.

Bill Smith, however, knew that wasn't the case. In fact, he knew that Estes and Jensen had not won *because* of the V-bottom, but in spite of it. "Estes and Jensen were in such a good condition that they would have won no matter what they paddled," Smith says now. "They worked all winter conditioning themselves, and those guys trained hard. They won that race strictly through the physical condition they were in."

Gene Jensen, incidentally, had reached the same conclusion.

Most of the Minneapolis canoeists lived within a mile of each other on the north side: Gene Jensen, Karl Ketter, Buzzy and Floyd Peterson, Tom and Phil Estes, and Billy Smith Jr. So the day after the derby, Jensen came over to Smith's house, which was a block away from the river.

"He wasn't celebrating any accolades or anything," Smith says. "He was right there. He said, 'I want to take a look at that boat.'"

Every day in the derby, Estes and Jensen finished first, so the next morning they started last. That meant every day, they passed Billy Smith and Bob Bergstrom. "They had plenty of time to watch us and our canoe and how much effort we were putting into it, compared to how much effort they were. And all the time his mind is going: *That's one heck of a canoe.* Because he knew that I was not in good physical condition at all, compared to those guys."

Smith and Jensen carried their canoes across an open field and down to the river. "He got in his canoe and I got in mine," Smith recalls, "and we paddled against one another. Then he said, 'You know, yours is faster.' That's all he said. He could see how good the boat really was. That's when he fell in love with it."

Jensen offered to buy it, but Smith wasn't selling. Instead, he told Jensen that it had a tendency to veer right. If Jensen could fix that, he could borrow it for the rest of the season.

So Jensen took Jim and Bernie Smith's canoe and worked to straighten it out, and he and Tom Estes took it up to La Classique de Canots, the race on the Maurice River in Quebec, which would become one of the "Triple Crown" events of canoe racing.

The previous winner of La Classique, Jean Lemay, had been in the 1949 derby but had dropped out on day four. And in 1949 Estes and Jensen won La Classique. It was the first of four victories there for Jensen, and the first of six for Estes.

The modern era of canoe racing had begun.

THE DYNASTY

1950

IN 1950, WHILE BILL SMITH HAD A JOB WORKING CONSTRUCTION, he fell off some scaffolding. The drop was only about ten feet, but he landed on concrete, was knocked unconscious, and injured his back. After that, he decided his canoe derby days were over.

Smith's former teammate, however, the speed skater Bob Bergstrom, spent the winter building a racing canoe for the 1950 race. He found a new partner in Olympic speed skating silver medalist Kenny Bartholomew. But at the very last minute, the Olympic committee ruled that if Bartholomew competed in the derby, he would lose his amateur status. Bergstrom went to Bemidji anyway to watch, and the newspaper called him the "saddest lad viewing the derby start."

This year, Tom Estes and Gene Jensen had once again been training all winter with their weights and pulleys. Now they had a new canoe with a mostly round bottom and lines that were eerily similar to those of Jim and Bernie Smith's boat.

This year, there were only three rules for a canoe: it had to be at least fifteen feet long, weigh a minimum of sixty pounds, and have a crossbeam of at least thirty inches. "The race is open to all models, kinds and types of canoes," read the official rules, and a June 14 news release said, "Metal, plywood and even birchbark will be utilized." There was a $40 entry fee (about $500 in 2024 dollars).

Predictions were that the 1950 Paul Bunyan Aquatennial Canoe Derby wouldn't be such a breeze for Estes and Jensen. "Half a dozen or more canoes, specially designed for speed," would be on the water, and they were "expected to provide the stiffest competition in the history of the race." After watching Estes and Jensen destroy the field in 1949, many of the racers had come back with V-bottom canoes. Even Jesse Tibbetts built one for Bob Tibbetts and Pat Murphy, who were racing. Jack Connor called Jesse Tibbetts's new V-bottom a "trim and tippy craft." Jesse himself said: "They can't even part their hair on the side to ride this one."

Harlow Thompson, age twenty-five, and his uncle Dick Peck, thirty-three, also arrived with a new boat.

"We didn't really like that [1949] boat after we tipped over on Winni," Thompson recalled in an interview. "We kind of figured we should have a different one. So we had a different canoe built in the winter of '49 by Bill Hafeman. You probably heard of Bill Hafeman. He built birchbark canoes at Big Fork for many, many, many years."

Their new boat was twenty-four feet long and made of cedar. Newspaper reports said it weighed 175 pounds, but Thompson recalls it being lighter.

"I don't think it was quite that heavy," he said. "I think it was 120-some. It was the heaviest and the longest one in the race. It was wood, with tongue and groove, and the wood was probably half an inch thick, so it probably soaked up water. With both of us in there, it only set about 12 inches above the water. It wasn't very deep. It was pretty shallow."

The bottom was "kind of a V," but not as deep as some. And it was fast.

"We had a speedometer on it," Thompson said, "and we could paddle about sixteen miles an hour."

Unlike many of the racers, Jensen and Estes didn't come back to the 1950 derby with a V-bottom. "We built three canoes last winter for this race," Estes told the *Star*. "We were trying to improve on the one we came in first with last year." Their new canoe was two feet longer, at twenty feet, and like Jim and Bernie Smith's, it had a round bottom.

The total purse was slightly less, at $6,000. But the individual places were mostly the same: $2,000 for first place (a little over $25,000 today), $1,500 for second, $1,000 for third. There was prize money all the way down to $10 ($128) for twentieth place. (Twenty-first, apparently, got nothing.)

Thirty teams signed up for the derby. Of the sixty paddlers, thirty-three were veterans of the race. Jim Smith, who was fifty, was paddling with Gilbert Jordan. Buzzy and Floyd Peterson were racing again, as was Tom Estes's younger brother Phil.

The Tibbetts clan had "steadily dwindled" over the previous two years, and only one team entered the 1950 race. Bob Tibbetts, twenty-seven, a former Golden Glove and University of Minnesota

The racers' names and canoe numbers hung on movable canoe-shaped signs through the middle of a massive banner across the front of Donaldson's Department Store in Minneapolis, 1950. *Norton and Peel photo, MNHS*

middleweight boxer, and Pat Murphy, grandson of 1928 champion Ben Tibbetts, bore the family torch. "To Bob remains the task of carrying through the Tibbetts name in this 1950 race," wrote Jack Connor. "But the whole Tibbetts clan was down on the shore of Lake Bemidji to see him off today, including the man who first talked the Tibbetts into competing in the 1940 derby." That was, of course, the "57-year-old Bemidji policeman," Jesse Tibbetts. "Throughout the years, old Jesse has been the guiding spirit that kept the Tibbetts boys in there paddling." Also present for the send-off were Tibbetts veterans Bud, Harry, Jim, Tom, Ray, and Elmer.

At the prerace sprint on Thursday night, however, things didn't look good for Tibbetts and Murphy. During the race, their V-bottom canoe "failed to show its speed." Rather, the sprint was won by Estes and Jensen, followed by Thompson and Peck, then Eric Hughes and Harold Westby.

Also cheering at the start was Jim Smith's wife, Theresa, along with their children Beatrice, eight, Roland, four, and James Jr., who was just eighteen days old. Jim Smith and Gilbert Jordan were one of only three Ojibwe teams in the 1950 derby. It seemed that the era of legendary Ojibwe canoe racers was coming to a close. The center of Minnesota canoe racing was shifting south.

On the morning of Friday, July 15, the racers gathered at Lake Bemidji. There were twenty-six teams on the line. It had been raining hard, but the rain stopped just before 9:00 AM. That was when "Governor Youngdahl raised a starter pistol toward the low-lying clouds and fired the opening shot," reported the *Minneapolis Star*.

The teams left at two-minute intervals, with Estes and Jensen in the last wave. After they'd all gone, a sad Bob Bergstrom "paddled out alone after [the racers] in his home built craft. And he almost caught up with the slowest team in the derby, too."

Within three hours, Estes and Jensen had passed all the teams but two. By the end of the day, they were more than fifteen minutes ahead of second-place Thompson and Peck. It was already clear which way the race was going.

On day two, Thompson and Peck made a push for first. It was a section they knew well, an eighty-mile stretch that "separates the 'sheep' from the 'goats.'" For more than seventy miles, the two teams raced bow to bow. But in the last nine miles, Estes and Jensen "staged a terrific sprint and gained seven minutes." They came into the finish "like a motor boat."

This year, the river was two to three feet higher, and the times were faster. Estes and Jensen were thirty minutes ahead now—eighteen minutes more than the year before.

By the end of the second day, only eighteen teams remained. The next day, three more teams dropped out. Karl Ketter and his partner, Edwin Knight, were cutting a corner when a tree limb hit Ketter, cut him over his eye, and capsized their canoe. They made it to shore, but the current swept their canoe downstream. After losing half an hour getting it back, they decided to scratch. Wayne Carlson and Donald Nims were also out after a log punctured their canoe.

Already the outcome of the race was clear. In fact, the dominance of Estes and Jensen would become a problem for the derby. Gone were the close races of 1942, 1946, 1947, and even 1948. By the end of the 1949 derby, columnist Charles Johnson had written, "The manner in which Tom Estes and Eugene Jensen . . . dominated this race has been amazing." But, he added, "The winning team's performance took considerable punch out of the attraction."

In 1950, their dominance again left reporters scrambling for news. Ed Shave wrote, "A very hot race is on for tenth position," in which teams were only two minutes apart. Jack Connor resorted to writing a column about how difficult it was to follow the canoes in a motorboat.

By the time Estes and Jensen got to Aitken, they had a forty-seven-minute lead. They did the lap forty minutes faster than in 1949, and it was clear that, barring some catastrophe, the race was in the bag.

Nonetheless, Thompson and Peck refused to give up. On the lap from Aitken to Brainerd, the two teams started together and "at no time during the 52 miles were they separated by more than a few feet." Estes and Jensen always remained ahead. But by the end of the day, they had gained only thirty seconds.

From then on, there were no changes in the position of the

sixteen teams. "The most excitement," wrote Ed Shave, "was furnished by Bemidji's gallant warriors, Eric Hughes and Harold Westby, who went all out in a driving attempt to gain ground on the second-place team of Harlow Thompson and Dick Peck." The two canoes raced bow to bow the entire distance, but by the end of the lap, the Bemidji team had gained only four seconds.

Meanwhile, the battle for tenth place was still raging. "Canoeists Practically Concede," said the Tuesday headline. "Estes and Jensen just too tough for others." "Nobody can catch them," said second-place Dick Peck. "They're just too good and we're not going to kill ourselves trying."

The places stayed the same. Bob Tibbetts hung on to seventh, just ahead of eighteen-year-old Phil Estes. Jim Smith and Gilbert Jordan were in twelfth, while the Mankato veteran Augie Schueneman was in last.

Sadly, Jim Smith had to drop out at Brainerd after his partner suffered "a groin injury . . . from the strain of paddling," according to the *Star*. Ed Shave commented: "It was a tough break for Smith, who was racing in his fifth derby and is one of the oldest contestants, being past 50."

With first place sewn up, news coverage focused elsewhere. The battle for fourth place: Buzzy and Floyd Peterson "poured on the steam." The battle for sixth: the Landwehr brothers held on to a two-minute lead over Phil Estes and Dick Mueller, who sprung a leak and had to stop five times to dump water out of their canoe.

And then there was the battle for last: forty-year-old derby veteran Augie Schueneman from Mankato was just ten seconds ahead of another team from Red Lake Falls. It was a friendly battle, and the teams "see-sawed back and forth in last place throughout the race." Schueneman, who had finished fifth in 1941 and third in 1946, wondered why he was even there. "I guess it must be this thing just gets in your blood," he said, echoing Blackie Jarnig's comment three years earlier. "I can't explain it any other way."

On Friday, July 22, the paddlers raced from St. Cloud to Minneapolis. Estes and Jensen made the lap in just over nine hours. After the racers reached the Hennepin Avenue Bridge, they were trucked around St. Anthony Falls for the sprint to the Franklin Avenue Bridge. "Thousands" of people lined the riverbanks to watch. Estes and Jensen won that too, adding the $75 prize to their $2,000 for winning the derby. Their total time was 55 hours, 57 minutes, and 34 seconds. They were just over an hour ahead of second-place Thompson and Peck, and they beat their own 1949 record by two hours.

Estes and Jensen told reporters that the race was "a picnic" and "a joyride," even at an estimated seventeen thousand paddle strokes a day. They said it was their "easiest race" yet.

Bob Tibbetts and Pat Murphy won $80 (about $1,000 in 2024 dollars) for their seventh-place finish. After the race, Jesse Tibbetts, "the Ball Club Indian dean of derbydom," was on hand. Jack Connor asked what he thought of the race. "In 1948 Estes and Jensen won with a Peterborough canoe," he said. "The next year, everybody went with Peterboroughs. But Estes and Jensen had a 'V' bottomed canoe they built themselves. So this year the paddlers went all out for 'V' bottoms. And what happens? Estes and Jensen win with a round bottom job they built themselves. There just ain't no justice."

"We had a good canoe, the river was high and we were in good condition," Jensen told the *Morning Tribune*. "Winning the sprint was toughest of all."

As they took their canoe out of the water, someone yelled: "Want to sell that canoe?"

"For $600 we will," answered Estes.

"You boys retiring now?" someone else yelled.

"Not if they let us enter again next year," one of them answered.

THE DERBY'S DECLINE

1951

BY 1951, ORGANIZERS KNEW THE DERBY NEED A SHAKE-UP, SO they eliminated the $40 entry fee in an effort to get more young people and university students back in the derby.

"The race . . . lost a large portion of its color, drama and public interest when these youngsters passed it up," wrote Ed Shave, adding, "if the race is to continue to have fresh talent, youngsters must be encouraged."

In another ill omen, Governor Youngdahl announced he would not start the race. He would be in Washington, where President Harry Truman was appointing him as an associate justice on the US District Court for the District of Columbia. "I've started all of them since I was elected," he said. "I'm going to be sorry to miss it." Instead he would send a representative to do his "chores" for him.

Even Gene Jensen was out. The three-time winner was stationed in Bermuda with the air force. (The Korean War had been blazing for a year.) But he sent his old partner, Tom Estes, a cablegram. It said: "It's all yours, Tom. Good luck." Estes was paired up with his brother Phil, and planned to keep the letter in his pocket throughout the race.

Three Ojibwe teams signed up, all with Tibbettses on board: Gene Tibbetts and Silvester Shotley, from Ball Club; Ray Tibbetts and Pat Murphy again; and Bob Tibbetts, who finished seventh the previous year, was paddling with Ken Prestige.

Harlow Thompson and Dick Peck—second-place finishers in 1950—had just won the Au Sable River Canoe Marathon in Michigan and were back for the derby in their twenty-four-foot boat, and they were in fine form.

"Pretty much every day after work we'd practice," Thompson remembered. "We were both working in the iron mines, and we had shifts. So we'd usually practice in the evenings. We'd run from Big Winni out to [Highway] No. 2, which was probably twenty miles. We did a lot of practice on Big Winni and Little Winni, in that area. And on weekends we would always go someplace to look and see what everything was like, and to check the river."

Karl Ketter was now teamed up with Buzzy Peterson. And Bob Bergstrom was back in the race too. This year, he was paired with his 1949 rival, Harold Westby. Augie Schueneman of Mankato also returned for his eighth canoe derby. He told Jack Connor that, at forty-two, he should be fishing in Canada with his old partner, Harvey Anderson, but again mentioned how "this thing gets in your blood."

Another old-timer racing was George Messing, whose late wife Dorothy in 1940 had been one of just two women to race in the derby. The fireman was fifty-six, graying, and wiry; his paddle was inscribed: "Ma-Pa 1940–1941."

The winners of all the major North American canoe races were present, as was William Williamson, from Toronto, the 1936 Olympic gold medalist in double blade singles sculling. Williamson had also won the Canadian and North American canoe racing championships.

Still, excitement about the race didn't seem as high as in other years. Dick Cullum wrote a column titled "Derby Can be Thrilling," suggesting that it might not be. "That special twist needed to light it up has not occurred yet and may not occur this year," Cullum wrote, "but it is due sooner or later. It may be that the strength of the team of Eugene Jensen and Tom Estes took the thrill out of recent Derbies. These two won so handily it was no contest. They owned the river. Nothing short of a floating mine could have knocked them out of the lead."

Now, for the first time since 1947, it felt like anyone's race. Jesse Tibbetts, the "dean of the Derby," remarked that "This could be the greatest competitive race since that first derby in 1940."

On Thursday night, July 12, teams gathered for the one-mile, prerace sprint. Thompson and Peck came in first, followed by Ray Tibbetts and Pat Murphy, then Ketter and Peterson.

The next morning—Friday the 13th—the paddlers toed the line for the start. Sadly, Gene Tibbetts wasn't there, because his partner, Silvester Shotley, had gotten called back to work in Minneapolis. Another team didn't make it from Michigan in time. And yet another Minneapolis duo wrecked their canoe in a car accident.

Minneapolis mayor Eric Hoyer was on hand, and he was invited to race against St. Paul mayor Edward Delaney. Hoyer declined because he couldn't swim.

As the nineteen teams set off, a strong south wind raised whitecaps on Lakes Andrusia and Cass. The tippy V-bottoms all took on water. Gordon Kossow and Harry Peterson, of Deer River, dropped out after their canoe swamped.

Karl Ketter and Buzzy Peterson had to get rescued after being hit by "an unusually big wave." But they got back in their canoe, kept paddling, and finished sixth for the day.

First across the line that night at Bena, on the south shore of Lake Winnibigoshish, were Thompson and Peck, followed five seconds later by the Estes brothers. That night, the Olympic champion Will Williamson told reporters, "I thought this race would be a breeze, but now I know better. We'll be lucky to finish."

The second day saw a fair amount of carnage. Ray Tibbetts and Pat Murphy dropped out at Ball Club, after their canoe started leaking, and "they were forced to spend more time bailing than paddling." Olympian Williamson and his partner were in eleventh place—almost four hours out of the lead—and "so far behind there was no hope of catching up." They dropped out.

While portaging around the Lake Winnibigoshish Dam, Bob Bergstrom slipped on a rock and got an inch-long gash over his right

The start of the Paul Bunyan Canoe Derby on Lake Bemidji, 1951. Canoeists are Dick Butler and George Messing of Minneapolis; Richard and Donald Meyer of Wayzata; and Tom and Phil Estes of Minneapolis. *MNHS*

eye. In Ball Club, a doctor put two stitches in it, and he and Westby resumed the race. Derby officials credited him seven minutes and thirty seconds for the time it took to put the stitches in.

By the end of the second day, there were only fifteen teams left. Peck and Thompson were "burning up the course." At the end of day three, they had a twenty-four-minute lead. Tom Estes admitted he didn't think they could catch them. Peck credited Bill Hafeman's twenty-four-foot canoe: "We finally got the boat now for this race," he said.

But it wasn't just the boat. They also knew the river in the winding section near Aitken and Palisade. "We had a couple of shortcuts that we took," Thompson said. "We did quite a lot of practice in that

Murray Olderman drew this panel of the 1951 race for the *Minneapolis Star*. The next year, Olderman would leave to become a nationally syndicated sports columnist and cartoonist. *Minneapolis Star, July 17, 1951*

area, so we knew it real well. Sometimes the bank of the river was only fifty feet apart from where it went around. So we cut through the bank in places, because as long and you had water, you could go through. It was legal."

Behind them, the field shrank. Russell Scott and Dick Mueller, who'd been in third place, dropped out after Scott drank river water, got ill with gastritis, and had to be admitted to a Grand Rapids hospital.

With only twelve teams left, last-place Dick Butler and George Messing were determined to see it through. "Well," Butler quipped, "we got in this thing, and we are going to finish."

With Thompson and Peck seeming "invincible," news coverage shifted to what the racers ate along the way. The answer, mostly, was fruit. Bob Tibbetts and his partner ate peaches and plums. George Messing and Dick Butler carried cans of tomato juice. Thompson and Peck ate "a couple peaches each and four or five plums, plus a bottle of water and a pint of coffee." The Estes brothers ate plums and a cupcake or two. The Canadian team ate one orange apiece, a honey sandwich, and heavily sugared iced tea. Augie Schueneman ate cherries and water. The navy team only ate chocolate bars and a lump of sugar. Ketter and Peterson had tubes that ran down into canteens of milk, so they could drink and paddle.

On Friday afternoon, the teams sped from St. Cloud to Minneapolis. When they got to the city, where "thousands of spectators lined both banks of the river," they portaged around St. Anthony Falls. This year, the final sprint was divided into three groups. The winner of each heat got $75.

As expected, Thompson and Peck won the derby and took home the $1,500 first prize, and they got to ride in the parade with the Aquatennial queen.

"We won a lot of things," says Thompson now. "I still remember the Atwater outboard motors. They didn't overpay us. But we didn't get into it for the money. If we had, we'd have had to stay home. It was just for the sport of it. People like challenges. That's what we liked: just the challenge. It was just fun doing it at that time. It was good people."

Thompson and Peck's time was 57 hours, 21 minutes, and 20 seconds. It was forty-seven minutes faster than second-place Keller and Peterson. The Estes brothers finished third. Bob Bergstrom and Harold Westby were fourth. Bob Tibbetts and Ken Prestige finished fifth, and got $200.

"It's one of those things," Tibbetts said. "You swear you'll never get in another canoe derby, but now that it is nearly over you look back and think of the fun you had, and the grind, and the crowds, and you wouldn't trade it for anything."

THE DERBY DENIED

1952–1958

ON FEBRUARY 19, 1952, A SMALL ITEM APPEARED IN THE *Minneapolis Morning Tribune*. It read: "Motorboat Race May Replace Canoe Derby." The new Minneapolis Aquatennial Motor Marathon offered $10,000 in prize money.

The next month, the Aquatennial board of directors approved the change. No explanation was published in either the *Minneapolis Star* or the *Minneapolis Tribune*.

In a 1989 overview of Aquatennial history, Catherine Mitchell of the College of St. Catherine noted, "During the previous years the same team had been winning the Paul Bunyan Canoe Derby, so the board decided to replace it with a $1,000 Power Boat Classic to be held in six communities around the state." There was no such announcement in the newspapers. The *Minneapolis Morning Tribune* said only: "Speed boat races will be held daily in Bemidji, Grand Rapids, Aitkin, Brainerd, Little Falls and St. Cloud, with a final race in Minneapolis."

It's hard to know exactly why the derby was canceled. It may have been the ballooning costs: in 1950 expenses came to nearly $7,000, which included sending "50 state, city and Aquatennial officials to Bemidji by airplane and auto to participate in the festivities." It also may have been that Estes and Jensen's dominance, followed by Thompson and Peck's, sapped the race of the drama needed to draw 100,000 people to the river. When Thompson was asked why it was canceled, he said (half-jokingly), "I think too many people from Deer River were winning it."

Or maybe it was simply a sign of the times. Canoeing—paddling with your hands and arms—had emerged from the ancient past, while the modern, postwar, industrialized world was defined by motors, chrome, and speed.

As a sort of consolation, Aquatennial officials signed off on an eight-mile Tri-Lake Canoe Derby. Racers would paddle across Cedar Lake, portage to Lake of the Isles, then end at Thomas Beach on the south side of Lake Calhoun. There was also a sprint.

On Sunday, July 27, the motorboat races were held on Calhoun at 1:00 PM. Then at 6:15 PM came the canoe race. Buzzy Peterson and Wayne Carlson won, completing the course in 50 minutes, followed by Tom and Phil Estes in 50 minutes, 45 seconds. Karl Ketter and Harold Westby finished third in 51 minutes, 20 seconds, and they won the half-mile sprint. All were veterans of the 450-mile derby, which was sorely missed.

In August of 1952, Dale Hennek of North Mankato (who had partnered in two derbies with Augie Schueneman) wrote a letter to the editor, arguing that entries in the 1951 derby had been depressed for several reasons:

1) Poor publicity in the run-up.
2) The increasing specialization of the boat needed to win. "The standard stock model canoe doesn't stand a chance," he wrote. "[W]ho has the time, space and money and most important, 'know how' to build a special canoe that is so tippy it's useless for anything but racing?"
3) The distribution of prize money: the first three teams got most of the cash, and the last teams could barely cover costs.

Another letter came from Bill Hilgedick, who raced in the 1952 Tri-Lake Derby, which he said was poorly planned, poorly publicized, and poorly run—but was still fun. Hilgedick felt "sick and disgusted at this half-hearted attempt of the Aquatennial's to keep the canoe derby alive." Either kill it, he argued, or don't. "Big Time canoe racing originated with the Derby from Bemidji to Minneapolis," he wrote. "The sport has caught on like wildfire in the Upper Midwest and Canada the last few years. . . . The Minneapolis Aquatennial has dropped the ball and Michigan and Canada are picking it up." In addition, a canoe race, no matter how unfair, is more egalitarian than a motorboat race. "When would you ever find a couple of North Minneapolis boys or Ball Club Indians walking off with the grand prize in a motorboat race? Instead of capital and machinery, the canoeist puts in muscle, back-breaking work and 'guts.'"

His letter prompted a response from A. B. Duellman, a vice commodore of the Aquatennial, who argued that the derby lacked "contestant appeal." He said the 1951 race had twenty-five entries and eighteen finishers (he was wrong on both numbers), even though they had cash awards for the first twenty-five teams across the finish line. He also claimed that organizers traveled to the towns along the route, and only one wanted to continue the derby. "In view of the lack of spectator interest in these various towns, we decided that if both contestant and spectator interest were dead, or near dead, it must be time to make a change. Regarding the muscle and back-breaking described by Hilgedick in a canoe derby, he should see the abuse the boys take in a speedboat classic, racing in the afternoon, taking their motors apart at night, and racing again the next day. . . . Regarding the 'guts' needed as described, there is more danger and excitement in one day in a speedboat classic than in a whole year of canoeing."

* * *

In 1953, perhaps in response to public outcry, a short version of the Paul Bunyan Canoe Derby was revived. The Anoka, Champlin—Minneapolis Aquatennial Canoe Derby would be a sixteen-mile race from Anoka to Minneapolis, with a two-mile sprint that started at the Camden Bridge. It was sponsored by Grain Belt Beer.

On Friday, July 17, the race kicked off the Aquatennial at Anoka and Champlin, towns facing each other across the Mississippi.

Eleven teams raced; an estimated three thousand people turned out for the finish. Wayne Carlson and Buzzy Peterson came in first in 1 hour, 56 minutes, and 55 seconds, eight minutes and nineteen seconds ahead of Francis Pumarlo and Russell Scott. Augie Schueneman and Dale Hennek finished sixth.

Columnist Charles Johnson lamented the lost race. "The canoe derby gave this midsummer pageant a kickoff that was natural," he wrote. "There were 10 days of buildup as the paddlers worked their way down the Mississippi to Minneapolis to the big finish. . . . The race gained national publicity for the city and Minnesota."

Walter Marcum, president of the *Bemidji Pioneer*, had been connected with every Mississippi race since 1928. He wrote to the *Minneapolis Star* arguing for the revival of the derby. "I do not know of anything that can produce more advertising for the state of Minnesota than this derby."

* * *

The derby grew a little more in 1954, this time to St. Cloud. The total purse was $600, $300 of which was the first prize. The race would be a two-day affair with an overnight stay in Anoka. A final, two-mile sprint would be held from St. Anthony Falls downstream for one mile, with a turnaround at the railroad bridge, then back up to the East River Flats.

Buzzy Peterson and Russell Scott, fresh off their victory in the Thunder Bay Midwestern Canoe Derby, signed up. Mankato's Augie Schueneman was entered. And Tom Estes partnered with Wayne Carlson. (They'd been fourth at Thunder Bay, despite a hole in their canoe.) Even Gene Jensen was back, this time partnering with Karl Ketter.

The racers left St. Cloud on Thursday, July 15. By the time they reached Anoka, just over six hours later, there were only forty-two seconds separating first-place Peterson and Scott from second-place Estes and Carlson. Ketter and Jensen were third, some twelve minutes back.

The next day, Peterson and Scott raced bow to bow with Estes and Carlson, all the way to Minneapolis. The two boats "sped over the finish line under the Broadway Avenue bridge in a virtual tie," but Peterson and Scott won the overall race—by forty-two seconds. They also won the sprint and picked up $100 extra, for a total of $400.

With the exception of Schueneman and his partner, all the teams were from Minneapolis.

* * *

From 1955 to 1957, there was no news of any canoe derby. But in 1958, the big derby—the 450-mile race on the Mississippi River—was back.

"Minnesota's once greatest test of endurance, the Aquatennial Paul Bunyan canoe derby, is going to be revived this year just as it was in its heyday when the event received international recognition," the *Minneapolis Star* reported. There would also be "startling innovations." For one, all the canoes would be identical, purchased and maintained by the Aquatennial. There would also be $20,000 in prizes, with $4,000 for first place (about $43,000 now) and $10,000 distributed for daily laps and other prizes.

The deadline for registration was May 20, but by February applications were already pouring in. "So many entries for the Paul Bunyan canoe derby have flooded the Aquatennial office that Ned Brandt, one of the prime motivators of the revived derby, Saturday indicated some elimination races would have to be held." These races would be on July 5, 6, and 7. Eighty entries had been received and Brandt expected a hundred.

Then on May 23, a small item appeared in the *Minneapolis Morning Tribune*: "Canoe Derby called off, Brandt quits."

There were few details: "Ned Brandt, general manager of the Paul Bunyan Canoe Derby Co., resigned yesterday for personal reasons. Derby plans collapsed with Brandt's resignation. . . . Twenty six firms that had made financial commitments will be given back their money."

THE RACE RISES

1959

THE NEXT YEAR, THE REVIVAL OF THE DERBY WAS ANNOUNCED again. This time, it was for real.

There would be $13,000 in prizes in cash and merchandise. Many of the big names would be there: Buzzy Peterson with Wayne Carlson. Gordon Kossow with a new partner, Howard Thompson (Harlow's younger brother)—both iron miners and cousins from Deer River, Minnesota. Dick Peck, the forty-two-year-old lumberjack and 1951 champion, was in as well. And, of course, Tom Estes and Gene Jensen were racing again. Estes had won La Classique de Canots in Canada two of the last three years, and the duo were as fit as ever. Even the old Ojibwe race veterans Jim and Bernie Smith, ages sixty and fifty-seven, couldn't resist signing up.

The 1959 derby was still mostly a working-class affair: racers included a railroad switchman, firefighters, four lumberjacks, a couple of guides, an electrician, a truck driver, a tile layer, plus some students and two salesmen. Tom Estes was working as a plumber; Gene Jensen was a cement finisher.

Given the past strife over canoe design, there were revised rules now: canoes could be of any material (most would be made of fiberglass), and they had to have a thirty-inch beam, be fifteen to twenty feet long, and weigh at least sixty pounds.

As before every derby, on the evening of Tuesday, July 7, a one-mile, prerace sprint was held on Lake Bemidji. The race went well, with a slew of newcomers placing high. Estes and Jensen, however, won the race by four canoe lengths.

But following the sprint, a major row started when the judges ruled six canoes illegal, including those of Jim and Bernie Smith, Gordon Kossow and Howard Thompson, and Dick Peck. The next day, the Smiths showed up with a standard model canoe and were reinstated, as were Kossow and Thompson, along with one other team. (Peck is not reported to have been reinstated, but he started the race, so he must have found a new canoe.)

But then the other racers complained about the "slim trim lines" of Buzzy Peterson and Wayne Carlson's canoe, as well as Kossow and Thompson's. They threatened to pull out en masse—killing the derby—if the two boats were allowed.

The Aquatennial president called a hasty meeting and offered to buy canoes that would meet the regulations for the two teams. Kossow and Thompson accepted the president's offer. Peterson and Carlson withdrew.

Estes and Jensen were "irked at the dissension" and also withdrew. They then immediately announced that their race-approved canoe was for sale. The Aquatennial president bought it on the spot and gave it to Kossow and Thompson. The two got in the boat thirty seconds before the gun.

The start had been delayed by an hour and a half, so it was already 10:30 when the teams set out across Lake Bemidji. Of the twenty teams on the line, a total of five would drop out by the end of the first day.

There was a strong northwest wind. The lake was rough, and the crossing was hazardous. Lake Winnibigoshish was even worse: the waves were reported to be six feet high. Race veterans said it was the roughest they had ever seen Big Winni. Three canoes swamped in the open water, including the one carrying former champion Dick Peck and his partner. They had to be towed in, which disqualified them. After that, there were no former winners in the race.

Another team, Norm and Mark Mohler from Bemidji, also swamped, but they were able to right themselves and continue.

Mark hadn't been in a canoe until half an hour before the race. Norm's partner had been ruled out by the medical exam, so Mark stepped in. They practiced for half an hour, then started the race.

Two more teams swamped while trying to come ashore at Bena in four-foot breakers. And one team waited three hours on the edge of Winnibigoshish for the wind to die. They crossed in the dark, finished at 10:30 PM, and were disqualified.

The rough conditions didn't bother Kossow and the younger Thompson in their new boat. At Cass Lake, they were already in the lead, and by the time they got to Winnibigoshish they were half a mile ahead. They won the first day's lap by four minutes and had only a few inches of water in their boat when at the finish.

Others weren't so lucky: One paddler chipped a bone in his elbow and couldn't move his arm. Another team, whose canoe had been disqualified, tried to paddle in a duck hunting canoe, but it was too slow, so they also dropped. By then only fifteen teams were left.

The second day was a seventy-six-mile grind to Grand Rapids through a winding maze of backwaters and oxbows. In every derby, teams unfamiliar with the river got lost on this lap, and 1959 was no exception: one team spent twenty-five minutes finding the main channel, dropping from fourth to sixth place. But Kossow and Thompson knew the river well and expanded their lead from four minutes to over thirty-three minutes.

Again, it was not a great year for Jim and Bernie Smith. They were in eleventh place after the first day. When they got to their home in Ball Club, they also quit.

That left only one Ojibwe team, Benny Tonce and Arnold Kingbird, who were loggers and guides, now in sixth. Two weeks before the race, Tonce had cut off the end of his left middle finger in a logging accident. When he reached the hospital, the doctor said he could sew the finger back on if Tonce could find it. So his wife went back into the woods, found the finger, and brought it in to the hospital. The doctor reattached it, and in some photos you can see Tonce's bandaged hand as he paddles.

By the time the canoes got to Grand Rapids, only ten of the twenty starting teams remained. Moving downriver, Kossow and

Thompson's lead grew and grew. At Jacobson, it was up to forty-four minutes.

The race wasn't close. The places didn't change. The lap from Jacobson to Aitken was reported as "an uneventful lap over serene Mississippi waters." Kossow and Thompson were now leading by fifty-four minutes. The only excitement was the eighth-place Mohler brothers gaining eight minutes on seventh place. Norm said of his novice brother Mark: "He's really doing a great job now, and we're getting better every day." Mark had no blisters and no muscle pain.

On July 15, the *Minneapolis Star* ran an interview with seventy-nine-year-old Ben Tibbetts, winner of the 1928 Diamond Jubilee race. "The field looks good," he said. "These boys are OK. The canoes, the river and the men haven't changed much since I raced." He noted that he and Bill Reynolds used a long narrow paddle with a squared end when they won.

On the lap between Little Falls and St. Cloud, winds were high and the water was rough. Portaging around the Blanchard Dam, Kossow and Thompson lost control of their canoe on a steep slope and nearly let it fall down the hill. Fortunately, the canoe wasn't damaged, but everything else was. "We broke everything we had in the canoe," said Kossow, "including our water bottles."

When the racers came into Sartell, three thousand people turned out to watch a special four-mile sprint to St. Cloud, as part of the St. Cloud Aqua Carnival. That too was nearly a disaster for Kossow and Thompson: they swung broadside and scraped over a rock in the Sauk Rapids. But after they straightened out, they powered on to win the sprint by half a canoe length.

Benny Tonce and Arnold Kingbird sprang a leak in their canoe at Little Falls, and on the way to St. Cloud it opened again. So that night, they drove all the way back to Little Falls, where a boat manufacturer put a six-foot fiberglass patch on it. They got only three hours of sleep, but in the morning they were ready to race.

By the time paddlers reached Anoka, Kossow and Thompson were one hour and thirty-eight minutes ahead of the second-place St. Cloud brothers Roy and Dan Landwehr. In seventh place were

Norm and Mark Mohler—on Mark's eighth day ever in a canoe. The Landwehrs were secure in their second-place spot, so they stopped a few times to smoke a cigarette and talk with derby fans onshore. They said they wanted to rest up for the final lap from Anoka to Minneapolis.

Their strategy paid off. The Landwehrs were the first boat into Minneapolis, beating Kossow and Thompson for the first time in the race, by more than two minutes.

In Minneapolis, the paddlers were trucked around St. Anthony Falls for the final sprint. This time, the iron miners blazed back for victory. Kossow and Thompson won the derby with a two-hour-and-thirty-four-minute lead over the Landwehrs. Their total time was 62 hours, 56 minutes, and 53 seconds. They got $1,500 in cash (about $16,000 in today's dollars), and a "paid-up life insurance prize of $1500 each." At ages thirty-five and twenty-seven, they were the oldest team in the field.

The Landwehrs won $1,000 for second place and two new "deluxe Crestliner boats." The third-place team won $500 and two Alumacraft fishing boats. The rest got cash prizes "plus merchandise."

Jesse Tibbetts was wrong: 1959 was not the most competitive derby yet. It might have been, if Jensen and Estes or Buzzy Peterson and Wayne Carlson had stayed in. Nonetheless, the race was deemed a success, and the turnout in towns along the river showed that the race—and the love of canoes—still had a power over Minnesota.

"There doesn't seem to be any doubt about it in Aquatennial officials' minds: there's going to be another Canoe Derby next year, and it'll be better in several ways," reported the *Sunday Tribune*.

Kossow, for his part, was in for another derby. "We'll be back next year," he said. "Everybody who finished this one will be back."

THE FINALE

1960

IN 1960, THE PAUL BUNYAN CANOE DERBY WAS ON AGAIN. Excitement was high, and this year's event would be one of the greatest derbies ever.

No one knew it at the time, but it would also be the last.

By the middle of June, fifty-two teams had registered for the race. Derby officials had secured just thirty-five sponsors and were calling for more. The sponsorships cost $385 maximum—about $4,000 today—if the team raced till the end, and $250 if they dropped out after the first day.

According to the *Minneapolis Star*, derby veterans were calling it "the cruelest race in the world." But this one would also be the richest: first prize was $1,500 (about $15,700 now), plus a three-day, all-expenses-paid trip to Las Vegas for four.

A total of forty-five teams registered. Among them were familiar names: Howard Thompson, the 1959 winner, was now partnered with Eugene Storlie (his and Harlow's brother-in-law) of Deer River, since his old partner, Gordon Kossow, had moved to California. Buzzy Peterson was back. The week before, Peterson (with Karl Ketter) had won the eighty-one-mile Flin Flon Gold Rush Canoe Derby in Manitoba, along with $1,000. For the 1960 Paul Bunyan derby, he was partnering with Wayne Carlson. Roy and Dan Landwehr—the 1959 second-place finishers—were also back in what would be their sixth derby. Phil Estes was racing too, this time with Francis Pumarlo.

There were no Tibbettses in the race, but Benny Tonce and Arnold Kingbird were back, this time each racing with their respective brothers, Frank Tonce and Dan Kingbird. There were not other Ojibwe racers that year.

Boney Selinsky, now fifty-three, was racing with his younger cousin Matt Selinsky. Boney (short for Bonaparte) took part in the 1947 and 1948 derbies, finishing fifteenth each time. He was a former semipro football player, and he had talked his cousin (who "wasn't so hot about it") into partnering. "The race gets in your blood," Boney told reporters, echoing the familiar refrain. "I've tried to stay out of it since '48. But this year, I just had to get back in." This time, the Selinskys would be paddling an eighty-five-pound fiberglass canoe, one of the heaviest in the race. In training, they had completed the run from St. Cloud to Anoka in nine hours. "That's too slow," Boney told his cousin, "We gotta do better. This is going to be a tough race."

A teacher named Stan Droogsma was partnering with Dick Mueller, a former Big Ten wrestling champion. Mueller had raced with Phil Estes in 1950 and Russell Scott in 1951. "When Dick said, 'Let's do it,' I knew what was involved," Droogsma recalls, at ninety-one, in an interview at his home in Maple Grove. "If there's something in your heart that says there's nobody tougher and better than me, then you want to go and prove that."

Mueller and Droogsma trained hard. "We paddled north on the Rum River for practice," he says. "And we got in shape. I weighed 165, and by the time we were done practicing, I was 155. By the time we got done with the ten-day race, I was 144. So that tells you what happens."

Last but not least, Gene Jensen and Tom Estes were back. It had been ten years since their most recent derby victory. Now the three-time winners were hoping to take a fourth title. They would be paddling "a homemade craft of wood and fiberglass bearing the number 16," wrote Jack Connor. The boat "looks like no canoe you ever saw before. Low at bow and stern, to minimize wind resistance, it suddenly flares out in amidship to meet the requirement of the 30-inch minimum beam. At 65 pounds it is one of the lighter canoes in the race and its lines are the essence of speed. Estes built the canoe."

There was little controversy over canoe design. "All the entered teams showed up and were certified without any of the squabble which occurred in last year's race," Connor wrote. The mood was congenial. Two students from a chiropractic school in Iowa had had their canoe shipped to Bemidji, but it never arrived, so Estes and Jensen lent them a spare.

On Wednesday, July 5, the racers gathered at 7:00 PM for the pre-derby, one-mile sprint, with a $300 cash prize (a little over $3,000 today). Estes and Jensen won the race in four minutes and fifty-four seconds—paddling around twelve miles an hour. In second place, "close on their stern," were Alvin and Walter Wisniak, ages twenty-eight and thirty-four. They were paddling "a special canoe built by Estes and Jensen," and were followed by Howard Thompson and Eugene Storlie less than a canoe length behind them. Wayne Carlson and Buzzy Peterson came in fourth, then Phil Estes and Pumarlo.

The next morning, forty-six teams gathered at Lake Bemidji for the start. Their canoes weighed between sixty and 105 pounds, and most were made of fiberglass. The sky was clear, with only a faint breeze. Governor Orville Freeman was on hand to fire the starting gun. The canoes started at two-minute intervals, with the Wisniak brothers off to an early lead.

Estes and Jensen started behind the first teams and chased the Wisniaks through the channels and across Wolf Lake, passing every other team along the way. When they finally caught the brothers on the far side of Cass Lake, they pulled up even and the teams raced bow to bow all the way to Bena. Estes and Jensen finished just thirty seconds ahead, though they won the lap by a little over seven minutes.

The second-, third-, and fourth-place teams all finished within a minute of each other. Droogsma and Mueller were eleventh. Three teams dropped out: one from heat exhaustion, one from cramps, and one—Dave Cline and Art Johns—cracked open their canoe on a rock.

The second lap was, as usual, one of the toughest: a seventy-six-mile slog from Bena across half of Big Winni—the most dangerous body of water in the race—followed by endless back channels. There was always fallout on day two, but 1960 was the worst ever. Reporter Jim Peterson called it "Black Thursday." Ten teams dropped out even before the start. "Blisters, pulled muscles, heat exhaustion and hopelessly slow canoes were the reasons given for today's failure of 10 teams to continue the race," Jack Connor reported.

The remaining thirty-three boats set off across Winnibigoshish. The waves were five feet high. Estes and Jensen loaded a twenty-five-pound rock in the back of their canoe to hold down the stern. They made it across, but other teams weren't so lucky: six boats went under in the waves, and were out of the race. Droogsma and Mueller had a canvas cover that shed water, so they also made it across and moved up to eighth place.

Next came the winding maze of backwaters before Grand Rapids. Droogsma and Mueller made two wrong turns and had to repass canoes they'd seen earlier in the day. "That kills you," Mueller told reporters at the time. "The emotional strain is the worst part of this race. Every time a canoe passes you it gives you a sinking sensation in the stomach. . . . I don't know why we stay in this thing. It's the toughest physical test I've ever ran up against."

Droogsma remembers it well. "We had passed everybody that day and were out in front," he says. "And I said 'Dick, I think we should go right.' He said, 'I think so too.' So we went to the right. Five canoes passed us before we got back to the main channel. We got in that night and went to the guys that were in charge, and said, 'That's dirty pool. We took the wrong turn because you didn't have it marked like you said it was going to be.' Dick really laid into them, and I did too. Then they threatened to throw us out of the race if we kept giving them lip."

Estes and Jensen won the day again, but Thompson and Storlie, in second place, had swamped on Winnibigoshish. They had to go to shore to empty their boat; then they got lost in the back channels. "We lost fifteen minutes trying to take a misguided short cut through the wild rice beds," said Thompson. They still finished the lap just twelve minutes behind Estes and Jensen.

Arnold and Dan Kingbird were not listed among the finishers on day two, with no reason given, but Benny and Frank Tonce were. They moved up from thirty-seventh to fourteenth place, and were the last remaining Ojibwe team in the race.

The heat was punishing—the temperature reached ninety degrees. One paddler collapsed. Another racer, Bob Gibson, was in sixth place when he reached forward to take a paddle stroke from the bow, passed out, and just kept going into the water. "I missed him when he went down," said his partner, Joe Stejskal, "but I backed up and managed to grab him. I got his hands on the gunwale and kept him up until we got to shore." Fortunately, there was Explorer Scout patrol present, and they helped administer first aid for "heat prostration." Gibson and Stejskal dropped out.

Droogsma and Mueller moved up to seventh place.

Roger Goyette, of Three Rivers, Canada, called their La Classique race "a little picnic" compared to the Aquatennial derby. He added that it was not only the toughest, but the best canoe event of them all.

On the lap from Jacobson to Palisade, Estes and Jensen raced Howard and Storlie bow to bow, pulling away only at the end for a five-second lead. That same lap, the Wisniaks moved into third, ahead of Peterson and Carlson, who'd run out of drinking water. Benny and Frank Tonce were also hitting their stride: they gained forty-four minutes and moved up two places into twelfth.

In last place were Dick Wagner and Ron Wicks, two high school students from South Dakota, with endless canoe trouble. At Grand Rapids they had worked until midnight at a sporting goods dealer, trying to patch a gash on the bottom with a piece of fiberglass; then they were back in the race the next morning.

At Palisade, more than a thousand people turned out to see the racers, while three more teams dropped out—one paddler had the mumps, and two had to get back to work if they weren't going to win any money.

Benny and Frank Tonce upped their stroke count to sixty-eight per minute, and "picked up considerable time on the rest of the field." It was reported that Benny's severed finger from the previous year was "all healed up." Now he had a "nearly perfect finger, complete with tip and fingernail." "I can go pretty good now with all five fingers," he told the *Sunday Tribune*. "I get a lot more power this year than I did last year." Benny and his brother Frank had been practicing up to eighty strokes a minute, and he'd lost twenty-five pounds training for the derby, running two miles a day in addition to paddling. By the time the brothers hit Crosby, they were in eleventh place.

On the section of the river between Palisade and Crosby, about half the teams were said to have taken "a flood control channel." The four leading teams, plus three others, did not. It's unclear if this was the "Aitken Flood Diversion Channel," a waterway constructed in 1957 that cuts off about twenty miles of the winding river. But the teams who took the channel were only penalized four minutes and twenty seconds.

Now there were nineteen teams left in the race. The leaders continued to lead, while at the back, several teams with no hope of winning reported that they were committed to finishing. Dick Wagner and Ron Wicks, the sinking South Dakota high schoolers, continued in last place. Hugh Cameron, a nineteen-year-old junior at Carleton College, admitted that he only entered the race to get in shape for football. He and his partner, Dick Jurvelin, twenty-six, were in seventeenth place and determined not to be last. "We found out one thing," Cameron said. "This is no race for amateurs. We only worked out for a week before the derby began."

The race was closer than any of the past several derbies. On the lap from Crosby to Brainerd, Estes and Jensen gained only eight seconds. Their lead grew from 23 minutes, 59 seconds, to 24 minutes, 7 seconds. The next day, they gained only another fifty seconds on Thompson and Storlie, with Carlson and Peterson just five seconds behind second place.

At Brainerd, Benny and Frank Tonce moved up to tenth. Benny told Jack Connor that he was hoping to earn enough to finish his

Benny and Frank Tonce, 1960. *MNHS*

third and last year at Mokahum Bible School near Cass Lake. In tenth position, they would earn $100 (about $1,000 today).

There was a Canadian team gaining on Droogsma and Mueller. Jack Connor asked Droogsma why they kept at it. "I guess it is the challenge of this race," Droogsma told him. "You want to prove you can take it, and by finishing you do prove that." If the two maintained their seventh-place position, they would win $250 (about $2,600 now).

When the racers reached St. Cloud, some four thousand people gathered onshore to watch. The two leading teams were neck and neck all day, but Estes and Jensen sprinted the last two miles and ended up fifty-three seconds ahead. Meanwhile, the Wisniaks gained a minute on Peterson and Carlson.

Benny and Frank Tonce usually camped in a tent, and Benny's wife, Josephine, cooked steaks over a fire for dinner. "We picnicked out like that because Frank is not used to crowds," she told reporters. But that night in St. Cloud, their support crew was late, so they had to stay in a motel. "It upset Frank so much he couldn't eat his steak," she said. As a result, when they got to Anoka the next day, he was so weak he could barely get out of the canoe.

Wagner and Wicks, in last place, had leaks in six places. The fiberglass patch they put on in Grand Rapids had split in two. That night they stayed up until 1:00 AM trying to patch it again, but the next morning when they were about to launch, the patches peeled right off. Josephine Tonce gave them some plastic stick-on patches, but those "didn't last ten minutes." So the entire fifty-four miles to Anoka they "had to keep dumping out water all the way down," Wicks said. Still, they were determined to finish, even if they had to swim their canoe to Minneapolis.

Despite the suffering endured by all the racers, there was little acrimony. No protests were lodged, and Jack Connor called it "probably the happiest and most harmonious race ever run." Even though Estes and Jensen won most of the laps (and lap prizes: two gold watches, two pairs of binoculars, two sleeping bags, two $50 bonds, and two cash prizes), there was little bitterness among the paddlers. "Those guys (Estes and Jensen) are great," said one of the Wisniaks—the article doesn't specify which brother. "They'll help anybody. They'll even pull your canoe out of the water for you at the end of a day's run if you're too tired to do it yourself."

On the lap from St. Cloud to Anoka, the competition was intense. The first four canoes were never more than a few yards apart. Thompson and Storlie came in ahead of the leaders, who were "nipped at the finish by five seconds." But Peterson and Carlson were the fastest on the fifty-four-mile lap.

The next day, on Friday, July 15, the racers left Anoka at 1:30 PM. There were high winds and waves on the twenty-mile stretch to Minneapolis. Estes and Jensen took on about twenty gallons of water in their boat. "We didn't know if we'd make it for a while," said Estes. The Wisniaks started two minutes ahead of the leader and remained ahead all the way. They were the first to land in Minneapolis. "We couldn't catch them today," Estes conceded.

The foundering Wagner and Wicks made it to the finish. As they crossed the line, their canoe—which had leaked for four hundred miles and was patched eighteen times—was three-quarters full of water. They had to pull over "50 or 60 times" to empty it. At the finish line, their canoe just sank. The boys wanted to let it go over the falls, but someone retrieved it for them. They said they'd be back next year if they could get a decent canoe.

Estes and Jensen won the derby, the $1,500, and the all-expenses-paid trip to Las Vegas. Thompson and Storlie were second, and got $750 and "a hi-fi set." Carlson and Peterson finished third, followed by the Wisniaks. ("[T]his is our first and last race," they told the *Morning Tribune*. "We'll never do it again.") Droogsma and Mueller ended up in seventh place and got $250. Benny and Frank Tonce finished tenth. Benny would go on to teach Ojibwe language at the Leech Lake Tribal College, which today has a Benny Tonce Drum Room and a Benny Tonce Memorial Scholarship.

Canadian Roger Goyette told the *Minneapolis Star* that the derby was "a dozen times tougher than our 128-mile race at Shawinigan Falls."

The 1960 canoe derby may have been the best derby ever. "Our reporters who made the jaunt . . . say that this was the best run and most peaceful derby yet staged," wrote columnist Charles Johnson. "There should be no doubt now as to the permanency of this grueling grind." He pointed out that along the way, there were crowds of as many as five thousand people cheering the race. "Many cities outdid themselves in hospitality and attention to the participants."

In another column, Johnson drove the point home: "It should be a long time before any one in authority in the Aquatennial will talk about dropping the Canoe Derby after the success of the 1960 back-breaker."

Johnson was wrong. There would never be another race like it.

The derby was done.

THE DEATH OF THE DERBY

1961–1964

ON JUNE 4, 1961, AN ARTICLE BY LONGTIME DERBY REPORTER Jack Connor ran in the *Minneapolis Sunday Tribune*. The headline simply read: "Canoe Derby Features Youth." The Aquatennial canoe derby would "make its run from Bemidji, Minn. to Minneapolis under a completely new format." Explorer Scouts would be the only contestants. The race would be 323 miles long, instead of 450—much of the first two legs would be skipped. It would take seven days instead of ten. "Each team is made up of eight boys paddling in two-man relays for designated distances before another two take over."

The cochair of the derby said, "This year's race will be dedicated to the youth of America and to their health and athletic advancement." Explorer Scouts age fourteen to eighteen would be eligible. Teams would use identical sixteen-foot aluminum canoes donated by Alumacraft Boat Co., based in Minneapolis.

No reason was given for the change. A cryptic note in the files of the Hennepin History Museum archive says the traditional derby was "stopped because of disruptive behavior," but there is no indication, in the news coverage or elsewhere, of what this behavior might have been.

On Saturday morning, July 8, 184 scouts on twenty-three teams gathered at Lake Bemidji to race. Norm Mohler, who had raced in 1959 and 1960, gave a pep talk to the Bemidji team. It was noted that he had appeared in several derbies "when they were run by professional canoeists." "If successful," noted another article, "the revamped one-week relay . . . could be the forerunner of national scouting competition."

Coverage of the race seemed half-hearted. Bemidji won the first lap. But the teams were faceless, and competition felt lifeless, with some troops there "on a lark." The most excitement came when Columbia Heights was "forced to accept unauthorized help when one paddler became ill." Several canoes also tipped on the lap to

Explorer Scouts at the start of the derby on Lake Bemidji, 1961. *MNHS*

St. Cloud; a few capsized in the Sauk Rapids. One scout was quoted as saying, "It wasn't the hardest job I ever did, but it was the most fun I ever had."

Fun as it was, the derby was no longer a contest among the best canoeists in North America. Now it was a carefully curated event for novices.

The team from Brooklyn Center won, covering the distance in 41 hours, 49 minutes, and 19 seconds, followed by Pine City in 42:28:37. There was talk of making the race a national event in 1962.

Gophers basketball coach John Kundla said, "They've given the race to the boys where it belongs. This is one of the greatest character building athletic events you could design for a boy."

"There doesn't seem to be much doubt about next year's race," Jim Peterson reported.

* * *

In 1962, the Explorer Scout canoe derby was repeated. More than a hundred racers took part. The launch was postponed by a day because of strong thunderstorms.

Because the Minneapolis newspapers were on strike for much of 1962, including the period when the Explorer Scout canoe derby took place, there's very little information about it.

And yet, despite the lack of public enthusiasm, the new Explorer Scout derby was meaningful to the boys who raced in it, like George Arimond, who went on to be a canoe racer and a professor of recreation management and therapeutic recreation at the University of Wisconsin—La Crosse. Arimond took part in the 1962 derby. He was on the Pine City team, which had a fierce rivalry with Brooklyn Center, which won the pre-derby sprint. After the race started, Pine City was leading most of the way, with Brooklyn Center in second. Then Pine City was penalized thirty seconds for beaching their canoes. Brooklyn Center won in 29 hours, 19 minutes, and 57 seconds.

"We were only twelve seconds behind Brooklyn Center at the end of the race," says Arimond now. "It was really close. Our coaches were just a bunch of dads who were just recreational canoers. But what we found out was that [Brooklyn Center] had a professional canoe racer coaching them.

"And that coach was Gene Jensen."

* * *

In April 1963, the Boy Scouts announced that the Explorer Scout canoe derby would be bigger than ever. It would attract national attention. By May, twenty-two teams had signed up.

On June 30, there was a story about how Florida scouts had a winter training advantage over Minnesota scouts.

The derby started on July 12. Again it was Pine City and Brooklyn Center fighting for the win. And Brooklyn Center won again.

* * *

In 1964, because of a conflict with the Boy Scout Jamboree in Pennsylvania, the derby was replaced with a two-day canoe race. There is no record of who raced, or who won.

"Officials emphasized that the 1965 Canoe Derby would be a full-scale event in mid-July."

Official emphasis was not enough: the 1965 derby was never run.

LEGACY

IT IS HARD TO QUANTIFY THE IMPACT OF THE PAUL BUNYAN Aquatennial Canoe Derby on the culture and history of Minnesota, or even of North America. But for more than two decades, tens of thousands of people around the state lined the riverbanks to cheer on the racers, or to watch the final sprint into Minneapolis. Hundreds of thousands more read the daily—often front-page—coverage in the major newspapers or listened to the race reports broadcast on the radio. So it's also hard to imagine a better way to raise awareness of the Mississippi River and of the canoe as a vehicle for adventure and exploration.

The derby stood at the crossroads of so many things. Poised at mid-century, it connected an older, nonmotorized world with a newer, more modern one. The race flowed though reservations and ricing territory, through cities and farms and suburbs, linking Indian country with white America. As such, the derby served as a neutral ground where people from different cultures and communities could meet in both competition and camaraderie. In the derby, the river became a rare kind of cultural meeting place.

The Paul Bunyan Aquatennial Canoe Derby was also one of the major factors in launching the late twentieth-century canoe-racing boom. The only canoe race older than the derby was La Classique de Canots in Quebec, which started in 1934. Winners of all the major canoe races in North America aspired to win the toughest race of all: the Paul Bunyan Canoe Derby.

The derby racers themselves—Buzzy Peterson, Gene Jensen, Karl Ketter, and so many others—would also dominate canoe racing across North America. And in 1961, the year after the derby's demise, those same people would found the Minnesota Canoe Association. For many years, the MCA published a magazine, *Hut!*, which documented the changing face of canoeing. Without the Paul Bunyan Aquatennial Canoe Derby, these racers might never have even met.

But of all the impacts the derby had, the diffusion of Ojibwe canoe building knowledge, epitomized by Jim and Bernie Smith's canoe, has been the least appreciated. It is the kind of technology transfer that fuels major leaps forward.

Gene Jensen, inventor of the bent-shaft paddle and other innovations, worked with Wenonah Canoe for many years after the derby to design racing boats. And while Jensen was certainly a canoe-design savant in his own right, part of his genius was also recognizing the genius of others. So when he saw Jim and Bernie Smith's canoe, he knew what he was looking at.

In the early 2000s, more than fifty years after Bill Smith raced in the Paul Bunyan Canoe Derby, he was in upstate New York visiting family. He pulled into the parking lot of a grocery store and saw a canoe on a car.

"I'd forgot all this canoe business," Smith says now. "And I looked over and saw this beautiful canoe. I said 'Oh my God, that's our canoe!'" It wasn't, but the lines of the canoe matched those of the boat Bill Smith had paddled in the derby all those years ago. "It was upside down on the car. I recognized it right away. It just brought back this flood of memories. So I said I'm gonna check this guy and see where he got it."

Smith walked over to the canoe. There on the side was a name he knew well.

In plain letters, it read: *JENSEN*.

JOURNEYS

BLUE HIGHWAYS

Two Friends Journey Down the Mississippi

EARLY ONE SUMMER MORNING, AN OLD FRIEND NAMED JD Fratzke and I met on the banks of the Mississippi River. The light was dim. The water was calm. Fish were making rings on the surface.

JD and I had grown up together on this river, further south in Winona. We'd both spent much of our young lives swimming in it, boating on it, and hanging out at parties in its backwaters. Now it was time to follow it.

I had biked down the river. I had driven down the river. But I had never actually *floated* the river. So I had the idea of kayaking from Minneapolis to Hastings, a thirty-three-mile trip, which I thought I could make in a day if the river was fast. When I mentioned this to JD, his reaction was instant: he'd always wanted to do the same. He came from a family of hunters and fishermen and spent nearly every weekend of his childhood on the river. He remembers one morning out fishing with his dad when he turned and asked why they never went to church.

His dad looked at him and said, "Don't you feel like you are in church?"

For those of us who grew up on the river, it flows through our minds and our lives, even though we can't spend aimless days on rope swings anymore.

For his part, JD was spending most of his time running his restaurant called the Strip Club Meat & Fish in St. Paul, where he turned dead things into delicacies. For my part, I spend too much time in my office staring at a screen.

To both of us, the river feels like a kind of refuge.

In 1988, it was recognized as such by the federal government, when the seventy-two miles winding through the Twin Cities were incorporated into the National Park System. Then in 2012, that same stretch was declared a National Water Trail in a new federal system, a subset of the NPS's National Recreation Trails.

This was a mere forty-five years after the Minnesota Department of Natural Resources had done the same, deeming all the state's 668 miles of Mississippi River a Minnesota State Water Trail in the country's first and biggest water-trail system.

Now, in the growing daylight, we stood on its edge, ready to set off. Next to us were our kayaks—mine a cheap, green plastic thing from Menards; JD's a long, sleek craft he called "Red Medicine."

Both, hopefully, river-worthy.

We pushed out into the water. The current was fast, and we felt giddy as it swept us past Fort Snelling. We veered around Pike Island, where the Mississippi and Minnesota Rivers converge.

From the trees we could hear pileated woodpeckers. In the water we watched beavers swimming up ahead. It was strange to be in the middle of the city, surrounded by so much wildlife.

Downstream we passed the Wabasha caves and paddled by a century-old wooden train bridge. We floated past St. Paul, then stopped to look at some barges full of rusting scrap metal. We eyed the heron rookery at Pig's Eye Lake and watched eagles perched on high dead branches.

We had only a rough idea of how long it would take us to get to Hastings. But really we didn't care. All that mattered was that we were back on the water. The river had receded after months of flooding, but it was still filled with whirlpools, unexpected swells, and powerful currents.

We both knew the river is never as calm as it seems on the surface.

South of St. Paul we stopped at an island to check out a campsite that was marked on our map. We beached our kayaks behind a fallen tree, then climbed up the steep, sandy bank and startled a deer, which bounded away across the island.

Through the trees, we could see the site was occupied. Two young guys were camped there, both of whom introduced themselves as Alex. The ground where they were staying was littered with beer cans, which made me a little nostalgic for Winona. It turned out they had just finished college and were on their way from Lake Itasca to New Orleans, a 2,350-mile journey.

We chatted for a bit, wished them luck, then went back to our boats and paddled on. JD talked about how he'd always wanted to do that same 2,350-mile trip—he wanted to know the river even better than he had. But life went on, and that window closed.

Instead he read books about it. We talked about *Adventures of Huckleberry Finn*, which he and I were rereading. We talked about Jonathan Raban's travelogue *Old Glory*, in which Winona makes a long, strange appearance as the author wanders about drinking with locals. We talked at length about *Canoeing with the Cree*, in which two young guys (not unlike Alex and Alex) just out of high school (not college) put their canoe in near Hidden Falls in 1930. But instead of going south, they went north up the Minnesota River, and on 2,550 miles to Hudson Bay.

We also talked about what may be my favorite river story, "Mississippi Drift," by a writer I knew, the late Matthew Power. Power boarded a raft in Minneapolis and floated down the river with a group of anarchists to Winona and beyond.

Above us the sun was hot, and we were drifting slowly. The river had widened, and we were paddling into a strong headwind. It was just after noon, and both of us had started to feel the miles: eighteen down, fifteen to go. My spirits were flagging. My nipples were chafed.

Just then, I came around an island to see JD standing under a towering cottonwood leaning out over the water. From a branch probably forty feet up, a barge rope hung down to the water.

We took turns climbing the rickety boards nailed to the trees, then swinging out and dropping in, feeling the weight of life lift, buoyed by sunshine and water and memories. By the time we finished, we'd almost forgotten how far we'd come and how far we still had to go.

Further south, we stopped on another island. In the middle, somewhat oddly, was a picnic table. So we hauled up our bags. JD whipped out a cast-iron skillet and a camping stove.

"If we're going to do this," he said, "we're going to do it right. We're going to have a true Huck Finn lunch."

Instead of catching and killing our own catfish, though, we just unrolled a brown paper wrapper and took out several meaty fillets. JD lit his stove, rolled them in cornmeal, and threw them in the pan.

"I even brought some watercress to make sure it tastes like the river," he said. Then he slathered the bread with spicy mayo, topped it with sliced tomatoes and cucumbers, and set the catfish on top of it all, like a tiny offering to the memory of Huck and Jim. It tasted a lot better than the river.

* * *

When we finished eating, we looked at the map. We still had ten miles to go, and the sun was sinking. So we packed up and paddled on, aching and sunburned.

Along the way, we talked about our families, about Winona, about how the river had shaped our thoughts, maybe even our lives. It was easy and natural, as if no time had passed since our paths diverged years ago before coming back together later in life. It felt good to know things that drifted apart could flow together again so easily.

The river turned east, and so did we. We pushed on through the wind, through the whitecaps on Spring Lake, and around the Nininger cliffs. Stroke by stroke, mile by mile. Pelicans filled the air around us. The sky started to go dark. Far across the water, the Hastings Dam came into view.

We paddled the last few miles in silence while the current flowed under us, until at last we reached the end. JD steered over and pulled the cord to announce our passage through the lock. A bell rang, and the huge steel doors swung open, welcoming us. We passed through them, and they closed behind us.

Slowly the water dropped, then stopped, and the doors opened on the other side. A little reluctant, a little relieved, we paddled out, both of us quiet, lost in thoughts of sunshine and water and of just how far the river had carried us.

UNCHARTED WATERS

A FEW YEARS AFTER MY OWN RIVER TRIP TO HASTINGS, I FOUND myself shin deep in the Mississippi again, strapping our family's bags into our canoe so they wouldn't float away if we capsized. Onshore, my wife, Bridgit, stood with our two girls, Libby and Josie, who were skipping rocks.

Once the last bag was secure, we climbed in and found, to our relief, that there were still several inches between the top of the canoe and the water. We pushed out into the river, and we were off on our journey southward.

This was an adventure we had planned ever since we'd moved back to Minnesota nearly a decade earlier. The town where I'd grown up, Winona, Minnesota, was 120 miles downstream from where we lived now in Minneapolis. Somehow, it felt important to connect the two places, to know the river between them. We would paddle together, like the voyageurs. We would forget about the modern world and its troubles for five days and see our home in a new light. It was just a small piece of the river's 2,350 miles. But it was a piece filled with meaning for me.

"We're doing it!" I said as we set off. "Let's paddle!"

Bridgit was up front, I was in back, and Libby, eleven, and Josie, eight, sat between us. It was the perfect time for such a trip: they were old enough to paddle but small enough that we could fit in one boat. We had this world-class wilderness area—a National Water Trail, part of the National Park System—running right through our backyard. All we had to do was get on it, and it would take us away. Fish nipped the surface of the water around us.

The sun rose as we rounded the first bend. It must have looked the same as when the writer Jonathan Raban took a motorboat down the Mississippi in 1979. The river, as he wrote in *Old Glory*, was "as big and depthless as the sky itself. You can see the curve of the earth on its surface as it stretches away for miles to the far shore."

We couldn't see that far, but we did have a sense of something powerful and unknown beneath us, that we were somehow putting ourselves at its mercy. Many people we'd talked to thought taking our kids on this trip was either dangerous or foolish. But to me it seemed like the real danger was never to have taken the trip at all.

Besides, we had even postponed it a day because of thunderstorms. After the rain stopped, I had come down to the shore and half-jokingly asked the river spirits for permission and safe passage. They seemed to be listening.

Between Minneapolis and St. Paul, the Mississippi flows through a gorge walled in by steep wooded hills and sandstone cliffs, so we moved fast enough that it barely felt like work.

"This is going to be no problem!" I yelled.

"We've only been paddling for five minutes," Bridgit retorted.

We passed under bridges and through the odd sideways currents created by St. Paul's spans and islands. Then the river turned south, and the screeching of the rail yard grew faint. The shore was lined with trees, and an eagle soared overhead. It was as if we'd managed to step out of the present and into a gentler current.

Almost on cue, we came to the island JD and I had stopped at with the giant rope swing. It was like something straight out of Huck Finn. We stopped there for lunch and took turns swinging out over the water like it was the 1890s. Then, reluctantly, we moved on.

The river slowed, but we settled into a rhythm and still made good time. Earlier, the residue of our lives—the phone calls, the emails, the deadlines—seemed to trail behind us in the water. But with every mile, these drifted farther away. By the time the sun started setting, all that seemed to matter were the water, the trees, and whatever was around the next bend.

We came to a series of small islands, one with a rudimentary campsite. There we set up our tent, made dinner, and fell asleep to the sound of waves lapping on the sand. Everything was going according to plan.

* * *

At dawn we packed, ate a quick breakfast, loaded the canoe, and then pushed off. The wind was still behind us. We passed an island full of pelicans before paddling into our first lock and dam. As we drifted in, walls of concrete rose some twenty feet around us.

The space was big enough for a barge, and we felt tiny inside. The gates closed behind us, and the lock attendant threw down a rope. We held on as the water dropped, revealing the algae-covered walls.

When it stopped, the lower gates opened and we paddled on. The sun was bright; the clouds billowed above. Thousands of tree swallows flew around us, eating mayflies and midges. Watching them and the other wildlife—baby turtles, endless eagles, a deer swimming across the channel—occupied much of our time. We told half-remembered stories and sang parts of songs. The girls occasionally got on each other's nerves. But most of the time, the river itself entertained us as well as any screen.

After a few more hours, we came to the Prairie Island Indian Community marina, where we stopped to use the bathroom. When we were about ready to move on, the wind started to blow, the sky blackened, and the temperature dropped.

"Maybe you guys should wait in the bathroom," I said, handing over the life jackets, so they wouldn't blow away. I put on my rain gear, tied up the canoe, and waited. Somehow, the storm went just south of us, and not a drop of rain fell. I thanked the river spirits.

Back on the water, we tooled past the cooling towers of the Prairie Island nuclear power plant.

As we moved downstream, I felt lighter, more unrestricted, more unburdened. Was this the freedom of being on the river? "Wait a minute," I said, "where's my life jacket?"

Bridgit's shoulders slumped.

"We left it in the bathroom," Libby said.

The sun was nearing the horizon. By then, we were a mile downstream. Everyone was tired.

"It's fine," I said. "I can swim."

We went on in silence.

* * *

The next morning when I woke up, the fact that we'd done no actual training for this trip became painfully clear. As a runner, I'd thought I was in decent shape, but now my back wouldn't bend in the usual way. Bridgit was holding her forearms like a velociraptor, massaging them until they loosened up.

The previous night, I'd jumped in the river to wash off. Now, I noticed red marks all over my legs and pelvis. (Later, I asked my dad—a dermatologist—about them. "Oh, that's just a duck parasite larva that burrows under your skin while you're swimming," he said.

"Just?" I echoed.

"Swimmer's itch. Don't worry about it. No one has connected it to anything bad so far.")

Itching, I shook the sand out of our sleeping bags and packed them, and we got back in the canoe. Today we would cross Lake Pepin, a windy expanse that everyone assured us was the most difficult part of our trip, if not the entire Mississippi. The lake was more than twenty miles long and several miles wide. It felt more like an ocean than a river.

First we stopped in Red Wing, where we bought a life jacket at the marina, then walked into town to get groceries. I'd driven through the town my whole life, but from the river, the city looked different. It looked foreign, almost exotic, as if it were in some other country.

Which, in a sense, was the point of this trip: to renew our appreciation for this place—an appreciation that would soon deepen.

As soon as we got back in the canoe, it started to rain. Back in the main channel, the wind pounded at our backs, pushing us along to where the river widened, and out into the open water of Lake Pepin.

I tried to steer us along the western side, but not so close that we got pushed into the rocks. The further we traveled, the bigger the waves grew and the harder it became to manage the canoe. Close to shore, we could see more eagles in the trees of a state park.

"I don't like this," Libby said, her voice quavering.

"Not many get to see the park from here," I said.

"Yeah," she said, "I can see why."

I didn't like it either. The waves were four feet high. Our canoe was too long to ride them straight on, and it was almost impossible to steer. The boat teetered on top of waves, and then dove into the troughs. Water crested over the edge into the canoe, and the girls bailed.

After more than two hours, we came to the narrow point where we had to cross.

"OK, we all need to paddle!" I shouted over the wind.

There were no boats or barges, so we turned and headed straight to the other side, a mile from point to point. The waves were still high and the wind was at our side. I dug deep to keep us at an angle.

We reached the far shore and turned south. Several miles away, we could see a smudge of land that was our destination, a tiny town called Stockholm with a campground on the beach. After a long, long day, we finally arrived just before 5:00 PM. We'd covered only twenty-one miles compared to twenty-six the day before, but they were hard-earned.

Our nerves were frayed. Our skin burned from the sun and wind. Our arms and backs ached. We found the camp host and asked if there was a restaurant in town.

"There is," she said and looked at her watch. "But it's closing in five minutes. Let me call and see if they'll wait for you."

We threw our gear in a camping spot and ran up the street. Inside, the restaurant was painted blue and yellow and had dollar bills taped to the ceiling.

"What would you like?" the waitress asked.

Bridgit answered for us.

"We'll take one of everything."

* * *

No one wanted to leave Stockholm. We were all tired, and we still had half of Lake Pepin left. The campground felt like an oasis, so the next morning, we lingered. I walked down to the beach and looked out over the lake.

It felt like weeks since we'd left home, not days. The time between then and now had been full and rich, not thin and fast—the way most days felt. A sense of urgency had fallen away, as if we'd stumbled on an older rhythm that had been there all the time.

But we still had fifty miles to go, and there were thunderstorms forecast in a few days. So once again, we shoved off. By midmorning, we'd reached the point where Lake Pepin narrowed back into a river. A few miles later, we came to Wabasha, the town where the film *Grumpy Old Men* had been set more than two decades earlier.

Onshore, we could see an ice cream shop. We debated whether to stop. To me, the dock looked treacherous. I argued that we should land on the sandy beach next to it. Bridgit said it was private. We had a brief, heated, pointless argument about this. By the time it was over, we'd drifted too far downstream.

Ice cream receded behind us, growing more delicious with each mile. The wind died. The heat rose. We had grumpy old canoers and grumpy young canoers. We continued without a word, all trying to turn our mood against the current. We stopped on an island for lunch, but there was too much poison ivy to do any exploring. We were beginning to know the river, and it was wearing us down.

By late afternoon, we started looking for an island to camp on. There were lovely open spaces. There were idyllic campsites. But it was still too early, so we moved on. Within a few miles, the islands became overgrown and impossible to land on. Ahead was a lock and dam.

"Let's just get through the lock," I said. "We'll have less to do tomorrow. It'll be our last day."

Without enthusiasm, everyone agreed.

The gates swung open. We drifted in.

"Where you guys going?" the lock attendant asked.

"Winona."

"You going there tonight?"

It was 5:00 PM. Winona was almost thirty miles downstream.

"Not tonight," I said. "Are there campsites below the dam?"

"A few," he said. "But they're a handful of miles down."

How many miles are in a handful? We didn't know, but given his familiarity with canoe travel, this didn't bode well.

Below the lock, we passed a defunct power plant with massive smokestacks that climbed high into the sky. The islands around it were choked with underbrush. We kept going—mile after mile—looking for a small spot to pitch our tent.

"Nothing," Bridgit said, despair creeping in.

She was tired. We all were. We'd gone almost as far as any day yet—more than twenty-five miles—and there was no end in sight. It was nearly 7:00 PM, and we should have been making our dinner.

We came to a grassy spot under some utility poles.

"We could camp under those power lines," I said.

"WHY WOULD WE CAMP UNDER THE POWER LINES?!" Bridgit yelled. Then, in a smaller voice, she added, "What are we going to do?"

"We keep paddling," I said.

Muscles tensed in her shoulders. Suddenly, she started paddling with a force I didn't know she could muster, powered by sheer rage. Water splashed over the rest of us. The girls looked back at me without a word, eyebrows raised. I put my finger to my lips, like we were in the presence of a wild animal.

Then, just as suddenly, she slumped forward in the canoe.

"It's OK, Mama," Josie said. "We'll paddle. You rest."

After a short while, Bridgit came back to life. We paddled another handful of miles and eventually came to a gorgeous, flat, sandy island. It was covered in white, paper-thin turtle egg shells. There was a small lake in the middle.

The day was over. The river had given us a perfect home for the night.

* * *

The upside of canoeing almost thirty miles the day before was that we had only twenty-three left. All things being equal, our final day would be an easy one, which would end with a shower at my parents' place.

The canoe felt light, and so did our mood. The sun was bright, and our minds were clear. For five days, we hadn't read a tweet, clicked a link, or sent an email. The weight of the modern world had lifted with each stroke.

At noon, we rendezvoused with Bridgit's father and sister for lunch by the river. The girls were offered a ride home but opted to keep going.

"We should finish as a family," Josie said.

We set off through the green hills. We stopped on a sandbar to let a barge pass. Late that afternoon, we came to the final lock a few miles before Winona, eager to arrive, but knowing that once we did, we would be stepping back into the torrent of our lives.

When the lower gates let us out, we came into the stretch I knew best, where I used to rope swing and water-ski and jump off bridges. Memories came flooding back. We passed under an old railroad bridge with graffiti from the class of 1989 (I was 1990), a kind of welcome home in spray paint.

Beyond the bridge, we came to a beach and pulled the canoe out of the water. It was bittersweet to be leaving the river that had carried us so far. We felt closer to it, closer to each other—and maybe even closer to ourselves.

But now, the trip was over and the currents of the present were pulling us back. For five unforgettable days, the river had kept the world at bay.

For that, and for seeing us through safely, we went down to the water, thanked the river spirits one last time, then turned toward home.

THE CANOE-LESS PORTAGE

"SO WE'RE GOING TO WALK NINE MILES?" OUR OLDER DAUGHTER, Libby, asked.

"No," I said, "only eight."

Actually, the Grand Portage, a trail at the eastern tip of Minnesota's Arrowhead, was closer to eight and a half miles. And by the end of the day, the four of us would feel every step of it, as travelers have for the past two thousand years or more, hauling their canoes and goods between Lake Superior and the Pigeon River.

Rising over seven hundred feet, the Grand Portage was the easiest route over the Sawtooth Mountains around the impassible Pigeon Falls. Once you got to the river, you could practically paddle all the way to Alaska, like a Minnesota canoeist named Jerry Pushcar did in 1975, on his three-year, nine-thousand-mile odyssey up the Mississippi from New Orleans, over the Grand Portage, then on to Nome.

We would be going only nine-ish miles, but regardless, there was no turning back. This was a trip we'd planned long ago, and now here we were—me, my wife Bridgit, and our daughters, Libby and Josie, ages ten and twelve—at the trailhead on Lake Superior at Grand Portage National Monument. We stood next to a wooden sign that marked the trail's start, hoisted our bags onto our shoulders, took one look back at the lake, then headed into the past.

The Grand Portage wasn't impossibly far, but it was impossibly cool: the idea that we'd be walking the same path used by Anishinaabe (Ojibwe) and Cree travelers, French Canadian fur traders, and British soldiers. In Ojibwe it was known as *Gichi-onigaming*, or "the Great Carrying Place." In French a "por-*taage*," as the voyageurs pronounced it (and Canadians still do), means a "carrying." In this case, a "big carrying."

The trail was a key route in the fur trade and the expansion of European settlement of Canada and America. In 1731, Pierre Gaultier de la Vérendrye became the first European to record crossing the Grand Portage. After that, it quickly became a bustling highway of trade.

"For a brief time," reads one national parks history, "this small piece of land tied together the fur trade of the west and the capitals of Europe and parts of Asia. And across its green miles, there strode a grand assemblage of traders, explorers, scientists, and financiers."

Yet even after that trade died, the route retained a mystique as a gateway to a vast wilderness. As Carolyn Gilman wrote in *The Grand Portage Story*, "To the first Europeans who ventured into this land, Grand Portage became another sort of boundary: between the known and unknown."

In a way, it still is. Or at least that was how I felt when I booked our National Park Service backcountry pass to camp for two nights on the Pigeon River at the site where Fort Charlotte stood in the late 1700s. To get there, we would follow in the footsteps of all those travelers who walked over the great carrying place.

Our girls had accepted the plan when we made it, but as we ascended the hill away from Lake Superior, they seemed to be having second thoughts.

"Why didn't we train for this?" Libby asked.

"It's not that far," I said. "You'll be fine."

Actually, I had no idea how long it would take us, or how hard it would be. We had camped many times but had never truly backpacked. All I knew was that we should be able to make it in a day. Besides, the voyageurs had carried ninety-pound packs of beaver pelts along the Grand Portage—sometimes two at a time. We weren't carrying nearly that much, though my backpack was starting to feel a little voyageuresque.

The trail was wide enough for one person. It climbed quickly at first, but not too steeply. The portage cuts through a gap in the hills known as the Grand Portage Highlands and runs straight through the Grand Portage Indian Reservation.

After about a mile, not long after we crossed Minnesota State Highway 61, we met a group of boys from a Wisconsin camp. They were taking turns portaging canoes at the tail end of a six-day trip down the Pigeon River.

"Are we almost there?" one of them asked, the desperation clear in his voice.

"It's about a mile," I said.

They thanked us and hurried down the hill.

Our camp was at least another seven miles. But we were still fresh, so we marched on, moving fast through the quiet boreal forest. Parts of the path were covered by boardwalks; others were muddy. We saw fresh tracks from moose and wolf, but encountered no other people.

After cresting the initial rise, the trail rose and fell. We crossed small creeks, until we came to a road on Abita Ridge that marked the halfway point—*aabitawikana* in Ojibwe, *abita* meaning "half."

It had rained recently, so the boardwalks were slippery. Both girls slipped and fell. Neither was badly hurt, but it marked a decline in morale. After about four hours and as many miles, we were tired and hot. When we arrived at a swamp—which the voyageurs had to wade through; we crossed on a boardwalk—we guessed we were at about five miles.

"How are we going to do this?" asked Libby, sounding a little panicked.

"We just keep going," I said. "There's only a 5k left."

That seemed to help. She had run a 5k race and could wrap her mind around the distance. But the relief didn't last very long in the heat.

"Do you think we're almost there?" she soon asked.

"Just don't think about it," I said.

She was silent for several minutes before saying, "If it's not around the next corner, I'm stopping!"

We came to the next corner, and it was not there. But she kept walking. She said the same thing a few more times before she really stopped, and Bridgit waited with her until she could pick herself up again.

Finally, after walking for more than six hours, we came to the riverside campsite. We threw down our packs and lay on the tent platforms staring at the sky. Our legs ached. Our backs hurt. I had bruises on my hips from my pack. We stayed there for a long time, until it started getting dark. A light rain began to fall, so we roused ourselves to set up camp and eat dinner.

We all slept hard. The next morning it was still raining, so the girls played in the tent and my wife read. I put on my rain jacket and went down to the river, which was only about twenty feet across at its narrowest spot. It was strange that this was the edge of Minnesota, the edge of America, and that the other shore was another country.

"Canada looks like the United States," said Libby when she came down to join me. Cedar waxwings darted out from trees on the shore. The sound of the water running over rocks was a balm.

Back at the campsite, we heard a thump and turned to see a fisher running through the trees. We had no cell phones, no link to the outside world. It felt like we were in a time capsule, as if a birchbark canoe could come around the bend at any moment.

The sky grew dark. The rain returned. I watched the campfire embers sputter under the drops, and thought of the countless fires that had burned here.

The next morning we made breakfast, packed our bags, and steeled ourselves for the trek home.

"Should be easier this time," I said. "We know the landmarks."

We were rested and in good spirits. We felt stronger. We moved faster. The trail wound through the forest, and soon we came to the swamp.

"That seemed really fast!" said Josie.

We kept up a good pace, and soon the trail started down toward the lake. We were cruising until we came to another rain-slicked boardwalk, where I slipped and fell forward, helpless to stop the momentum of my massive pack. In slow motion, it pushed me down. With trekking poles in my hands, I could see the wood approaching my face, but all I could do was tilt my head down to avoid breaking my nose. My forehead bore the brunt of the blow. I lay unmoving for several seconds.

"Are you OK, Daddy?" Josie asked.

"I think so," I said, struggling to my feet. Each family member cringed at the lump that was already starting to protrude from my head.

But we had to go on.

Downhill toward the big lake we went. We were practically running by the time we reached the trailhead, where the wide waters of Lake Superior opened before us. Once we arrived, we stood there for a minute, dropped our packs, and lay in the grass, happy to reach the end of our Grand Portage.

DEAD COLD

THE SKY WAS STILL DARK ON A SUNDAY MORNING IN LATE March of 2021 when I set my new solo canoe on the surface of the Mississippi River. I'd been thinking about this moment for years, dreaming of all the places I could paddle once I got this boat. Now, I was finally ready to launch on its maiden voyage.

I strapped my dry bag onto the crossbar, checked my pocket for my phone (which was also in a small dry bag), and waded into the river in my rubber boots, just north of the Ford Parkway Bridge between Minneapolis and St. Paul. I slid the boat out. When I stepped in, I noticed that it felt unsteadier than boats I was used to. Then I sat down, started paddling, and forgot about it.

Spring had come early. The temperature the week before had been in the seventies, and the snow and cold felt like a distant memory, even though a week or so before ice floes had drifted past here. I knew the water was cold, but that seemed like more of an inconvenience than a threat. Besides, after the first pandemic winter, I was desperate to get outside.

The sun was rising. I paddled up the gorge section of the Mississippi, which runs between the high banks of the Twin Cities, with hills—cliffs, almost—on either side. To the east side, an owl called. From the west, another answered. I was in the middle of the city, but also very far from it.

Although I was a fairly experienced canoeist, I'd never owned, or even paddled, a solo canoe. I'd been to the Boundary Waters Canoe Area Wilderness many times, and I'd worked as the trips director for a YMCA camp in northern Minnesota. A few years earlier, my wife and two daughters had paddled down 125 miles of the Mississippi together on a five-day trip.

I was careful. I always stepped along the midline. In all that time, I'd never tipped a canoe, and I had no reason to expect today would be any different.

The air temperature was thirty-one degrees, but it didn't feel that cold. As I made my way upstream the wind started gusting out of the northwest, though I was protected by the west bank. I moved along, making good time, staying close to shore. But when I came to the Lake Street Bridge, I decided to go around a footing in the middle of the river before heading downstream.

As I moved out into the main channel, the wind grew stronger. The canoe was light Kevlar, and as I tried to paddle left, it kept blowing me right. So I reached out for a big "C" stroke to correct my course. As I did this, the bow came up, and the wind seemed to catch it from underneath. Before I knew what was happening, the canoe was tipping slowly at first, then faster. I tried to shift my weight back to the middle but was too late. I was past the point of no return. I looked up at the underside of the bridge as I sank sideways into the cold water.

Submerged to my neck, I was shaken but still calm.

"OK," I said out loud, "just get to shore."

I knew this was dangerous, but I didn't know how dangerous. I'd never heard of "cold shock." I didn't know about the "mammalian diving reflex," where cold water on your face causes blood to move out of your arms and legs to your core. I didn't know that in waters this cold, I only had between five and twenty minutes before my body started shutting down.

In fact, most of what I knew came from an essay I'd read long ago by David Quammen called "The Big Chill." It was about a troop of Boy Scouts who had tipped their canoes in a glacier-filled lake. They all died. Quammen thought hypothermia had killed them, but the autopsy concluded they'd drowned. Quammen tried, and failed, to answer the riddle of which one had really ended their lives—the cold or the water.

Now, years later, I was about to come face-to-face with the answer.

I grabbed my paddle and swam. I held my canoe and kicked for shore. A mile or so downstream was a dam, so I knew if I let go of the canoe it would be destroyed, which at that point was still my greatest fear. But it was already too hard to pull, so I pushed it ahead of me. My boots kept slipping off, and each time I tried to pull them back on. Because how—was the small question in my mind—could I walk down the rock shore without boots?

Such are the mistakes we make in our final moments.

My body temperature dropped. My right boot slipped off one last time. I let it go, and it was gone. "Get to shore," I told myself, trying to focus on the one thing that mattered. "Just get to shore."

I made some progress. The bank got closer, but it was still at least fifty feet away. It wasn't enough. I kicked harder. I pushed the canoe. After about ten minutes I started getting tired. My face dipped under the water. As a strong swimmer, this alarmed me. I had a life jacket on, but my armpits hung on the straps while I struggled to keep my head up.

My limbs felt heavy. Water came over my chin, into my mouth. Everything felt hard now. Then, in a moment of clarity, a thought came into my head. It was not a question. It was not a possibility. It was not panic. It was just a fact, solid as a stone: I am not going to make it to that shore.

It was around 7:00 AM on a Sunday in March on the Mississippi River. I hadn't seen another soul on the water. But suddenly there was a flash of red in the corner of my eye. It was another canoe, coming toward me. In it sat two young men. The one in the bow had a coiled rope with a float attached. They already knew I was in trouble.

"Can you guys help me?" I yelled.

He threw the rope. "How long have you been in here?" he asked.

"Not long," I said, without really knowing, except that it had been too long.

He handed the rope to his friend in the stern and started paddling toward shore. "Don't worry about your canoe," he said. "We'll get it."

I let the boat go. The man in front paddled, while the one in back held the rope. I spied a small loop on the back of the boat and pulled myself closer. "I can hold this," I said, and grabbed the loop.

Even with two paddlers, the current was hard to plow through. But eventually we got there. I felt my foot touch the muddy bottom, and I climbed out with one boot and one sock, then dragged myself onto shore. I turned back to them.

"Thanks, you guys. You're a lifesaver," I said, then added, "Literally."

They turned downstream to retrieve my canoe, which was already far away. Onshore, I pulled my phone out of its dry bag and called my wife. She could tell something was wrong.

"Where are you?"

I told her what happened, and asked her to come. "Turn the heat on high," I said.

I could see the men pulling my canoe onto a beach downriver. I knew I needed to get warm, so I started running down the rocky trail, over culverts, through the woods, until I came to the paddlers. I couldn't feel anything on my bootless foot.

"We put your canoe up on the beach," the man in front shouted.

"Thanks, you guys," I said. "I really don't know what I would have done if you hadn't shown up." I didn't know what else to say. How do you thank someone for saving your life?

"My name's Jake," he called.

"And I'm Hunter," said the man in back.

I thanked them again. They asked if I needed a ride, but I told them someone was coming. They waved and paddled back upstream. I ran down the trail, found my canoe, hoisted it onto my shoulders, and ran up the stone stairs to the road, powered by fear and adrenaline.

When I got to the top, my wife and two daughters pulled up. They opened the back of our minivan. My limbs were stiff, but I climbed in the back and started peeling off wet clothes. The water temperature, I later learned, was around forty-two degrees. My core temperature was probably in the eighties. Once in the van, my whole body started shaking. The heat was blasting, but I couldn't feel it at all.

Back home I drew a hot bath and stayed in it for an hour and stared at the ceiling. And as I lay there, a similar scenario was unfolding to the south. Just outside of Ames, Iowa, a college crew team made up of two young men and three women were rowing on a small lake when the wind—the same wind that tipped me—came up suddenly and flipped their boat.

The students tried to hold on to their boat, but the waves were too violent. They tried to swim too. Two girls were rescued by locals in kayaks. One girl made it most of the way to shore and was pulled out. Both young men died.

To answer Quammen's question: when you die in cold water, it's not either hypothermia or drowning. It's both. Hypothermia paralyzes you. Then you drown.

* * *

The next day, my fingers ached from the cold. My head felt thick, but at the same time my thoughts raced. I pored over the details of what had happened: the way the canoe had tipped, slowly, then quickly; the shock of the freezing water; the struggle to get to shore. The sudden knowledge that I wouldn't.

Then the red canoe.

The two young men.

The rope.

The second chance.

I ran this chain of events on a loop, cataloging my mistakes and miscalculations. I tried to stitch together a version of the story in which there was a good reason those two had arrived at that exact moment. But no matter how I moved the pieces of the puzzle, they refused to take that shape.

For weeks I felt in limbo between two timelines: the one where I'd lived, and the one where I hadn't. My mind toggled back and forth. I kept thinking about those college kids, about how lucky I was, about Hunter and Jake. I woke up at night running through the events, examining the mistakes and miscalculations I hadn't known I was making. I had nightmares. I was treading water, the shore in sight, knowing I would never make it.

It was nearly a month before I could accept the arbitrary terms of my survival. By then, the episode began to feel like something that had happened, rather than something that was still happening.

One thing I never forgot, though, was my rescuers. Who were they? What were they doing on the river at 7:00 AM in March? How did our paths converge at the last possible minute? Whenever I biked across the river, I looked down for a splash of red. But they were never there. At home, the internet just told me there were lots of hunters named Jake.

* * *

A year later, I published a story about the experience in the Minneapolis paper, the *Star Tribune*. It was embarrassing to put the whole affair—the foolishness, the hubris, the dumb luck—out in the world. But if it saved a life, I thought, a little embarrassment was worth it. Besides, there was a small chance someone who read it might know my rescuers.

The story went viral. It raced through the swollen streams of social media, racking up huge page views. Emails started to pour in, from friends, from strangers, from people who'd lost loved ones to cold water, and from those who'd nearly lost themselves.

Then, an email arrived:

> Hi Frank,
>
> Hunter and I read the story you wrote in the *Star Tribune* today. We also think about this experience quite often, we've wondered if we would cross paths with you at some point. After all, South Minneapolis isn't that big. Would you want to grab a drink sometime? Would be great to meet under better circumstances.
>
> Best,
> Jake and Hunter

Not long after that, we met at a bar within a mile of the river. I arrived early. Sitting in a booth, I felt oddly nervous. A few minutes later, the two walked in. We embraced like old friends.

They were taller than I expected. Jake, it turned out, worked for the federal government, though the year before he'd still been in grad school. Hunter was a hydrologist with the Minnesota Department of Transportation.

We sat down and ordered drinks while they told me their story.

For a few years, the two had been paddling the Mississippi in sections. After a long pandemic winter, they were eager to be out on the river. They'd planned to go later in the day, but Jake had to get back for a meeting, so they decided to go at dawn. As they were getting ready, Hunter, a whitewater kayaker, grabbed his "throw line" for rescues.

"I figured we had it, and it's cold water," he said. "So I threw it in at the last minute."

Hunter picked up Jake around 6:30. By 6:45, they were at the Bohemian Flats landing near the University of Minnesota. Once on the water, they had a tailwind and sped downstream.

Near the Lake Street Bridge, they saw something up ahead. They thought it might be a log, but as they got closer they could see it was a canoe.

At first, they couldn't see anyone in the water. Then they saw me, but couldn't tell if I was alive. When they got closer, they could see I was trying to make it to shore.

"When I saw you," Hunter said, "I thought, *He's not going to make it*."

They knew the risk that a drowning person will swamp a rescue boat. After discussing this, they agreed if I got too close, they'd drop the line to keep all three of us from dying.

From the bow, Jake threw the rope. When they turned toward shore, he handed the line back to Hunter. By then, I was close to the stern. I saw a loop of rope drilled through the end of the boat.

"I can just hold this," I said. Hunter paused, and looked at the loop like he was trying to make a decision. But when I grabbed the loop, the boat stayed steady, so he picked up his paddle and helped power the boat through the spring current toward shore.

When my feet finally touched the mud, I climbed out while they hurried downstream to get my canoe. After calling home, I ran after them. Down the shore, we met and exchanged names. They also asked if I was OK. I said I was, and that my wife was coming. Then I ran down to get my canoe, and they paddled on.

Later, they regretted not staying to make sure I was actually all right. But I was running down the shore, and it seemed like there was nothing left to do. So they left.

For them, the day felt different now. They talked over the incident as they paddled on, the magnitude of it sinking in. Then they went to shore, portaged up the steep bank, and jogged back to get their car. They talked about it for the rest of the day.

Back home, they also read about the two college kids in Iowa who died that morning in cold water. "We knew it was a close call," Jake told me, "but reading about the crew team later that day, it was like, *Oh, wow, this truly can kill people*."

The experience affected them deeply, and they struggled to make sense of it. Hunter said some people heard the story like a lesson in heroism. But he didn't see it that way. They didn't feel like heroes. For him, it was more about strange timing, or maybe something like fate. "For a couple weeks," he said, "if not a couple months, I thought about it quite a bit. One thing I couldn't get over is how we ended up being on the river at that time. It was just this random sequence of events that led to us getting up at 6:30 in the morning on Sunday to go paddle, which is not a normal thing for me to do."

"What are the odds that we would have been there?" asked Jake. "It just didn't make sense. I still have a hard time wrapping my head around it. It just seems like we were supposed to be there."

None of us knew quite what to make of the convergence, but I felt a deep gratitude for it. We stayed at the bar and talked for a long time: about canoeing, about the river, about their jobs and their families. Hunter had a two-year-old and another on the way.

We talked about things you don't get to do when you drown in a river.

Finally, it was time to leave. As we stood up, Hunter made a suggestion. "We should go paddling sometime."

"When it warms up," Jake added.

I thought about the river, about the water, about the way things come together.

"Yeah," I said. "I would love that."

LET IT FLOW

Racing the River

I'D BEEN PADDLING FOR ALMOST SEVEN HOURS WHEN THE explosions started.

BOOM!!!

I jumped. Then I remembered that Camp Ripley, the expansive military base that lines the Mississippi River, was on my right. A nighttime artillery exercise had evidently begun.

BOOM!!!

In the darkness I couldn't see much except for the distant lights of my fellow competitors in the MR150, a marathon canoe race from Brainerd to Coon Rapids in its second year.

BOOM!!!

The explosions kept coming. Some felt far away. Others were unsettlingly close. Parachute flares occasionally lit up the sky, allowing me to see the river ahead. When these burned out, everything went dark. I turned on my headlamp to scan the water, but all I could see was a blizzard of flying insects, like when you turn on your car's brights in a snowstorm.

Bombs weren't what I expected when I signed up for the MR150. Then again, I didn't know exactly what to expect, or how long it would take me to paddle 150 miles.

My boat was a small Wenonah canoe, made of Kevlar. It wasn't built for racing, but it was decently fast and light enough to carry over the race's six portages. I figured I could make it before the fifty-hour cutoff, when the race ends whether you've finished or not.

I mean, how hard could it be?

The year before, a friend and I had competed in the inaugural MR48, a race from Clearwater to Coon Rapids. We did virtually no training, other than paddling together a few times, and the race was a fun ride down a fast river. The only mishap came around mile thirty, when my partner dropped his TUMS in a puddle in the canoe. I reached forward to grab the bottle and pulled an ab. After I caught my breath, we paddled on and even got a second-place trophy.

So I figured, *Why not take it up a notch?* and signed up for this race as a solo canoeist. Based on our performance in the MR48, I had illusions of doing well. I even imagined myself on a podium—or at least with a respectable thirty-ish-hour finish.

The MR150 is the brainchild of Scott Miller and Todd Foster, cofounders of Two Paddles Canoe & Kayak Races, which hosts the Mississippi River Paddle Weekend each June. In addition to the 48- and 150-mile races, there are shorter races of 5, 10, and 25 miles.

The 2023 MR150 started on Friday, June 9, at 3:00 PM and had a cutoff time of Sunday, June 11, at 5:00 PM. Whatever happened in between—sleep, food, water, forward movement, bodily functions—was up to the racer and their support crew. I did not have a support crew, so it was up to me.

The entrants in the MR150 ran the gamut. Their ages ranged from sixteen to seventy-five years, and they came from thirteen states and three Canadian provinces. There were middle-aged men from Minnetonka who didn't train at all. There was a family from Grand Forks who brought, for some reason, fly swatters. There were two "Boundary Waters boys" from Ely, one of whom had raced in the Yukon 1000, a thousand-mile race, the prior year. And there were serious paddlers who had traveled from as far away as California and Quebec, including the previous year's winner from Illinois.

They paddled everything from Gene Jensen–designed racing canoes, to Kevlar touring boats, to long kayaks, to stand-up paddleboards, to the insanely fast kayak-like craft called surfskis favored by the top racers. There was even one good old-school Alumacraft canoe.

Around 2:45, at Brainerd's Lum Park, we started pushing our boats into the water. I drifted out and found myself near the front.

At 3:00 PM, Miller counted down and blew the horn. The race was on!

Someone rammed me from behind and turned me sideways. By the time I got straightened out, I was nearly in last place. My dreams of glory receded as fast as the surfskis disappearing around the bend.

* * *

Later that night, the explosions and flares tapered off. The sky was a dull gray that reflected on the water. I let my eyes adjust to the light and peered ahead, trying to see the river. The water level was extremely low, and rocks were everywhere.

I slalomed around the ones I could see and *scraaaaped* across the ones I couldn't. I got hung up and spun around on others. Some racers, I would later learn, had to get out and walk their boats, but mine was light enough to pass over most of it.

The low water lasted all the way to the Little Falls Dam, where I arrived around 2:30 AM. Onshore at the portage, I asked the race volunteers if I could lie in the grass while they watched my gear. They offered me a chair, which I gladly accepted. I dozed in it for an hour, woken occasionally by the sounds of other boats pulling in and passing me. By the time I loaded up to leave, I was firmly in last place.

* * *

The MR150 is not the first marathon race on the Mississippi River. First there was the Mississippi Marathon in 1919, then the 500-mile Diamond Jubilee Marathon in 1928, and of course the 450-mile Paul Bunyan Canoe Derby from 1940 to 1963. After that, there were other, shorter races.

The derby, however, was the toughest. As I paddled the MR150, I remembered Benny Tonce, the Ojibwe paddler who, in 1959, had

had his finger chopped off in a logging accident two weeks before the race, then sewn back on. He raced anyway.

Thinking about Tonce, and about all the Mississippi paddlers over the centuries, made me feel like part of something bigger than just the MR150. We were all linked by the pull of the river. In an era when so many things change so fast, it felt good to be doing something almost timeless.

Day and night, year in and year out, the river always flows.

* * *

Dawn was like a tonic. I'd slept for only an hour, but I now felt alive. I felt hopeful. I felt like I could do this. There were only a hundred miles left!

The river was beautiful in the morning light. It seemed wild and free. I saw huge softshell turtles sunning themselves. I watched a beaver tow a branch upstream. From shore, a wolf pack howled.

At midmorning I pulled into Mississippi River County Park in Stearns County, where I took a break and promptly fell asleep on a picnic table. After about fifteen minutes I woke up, got back in my canoe, and started downstream again.

The next forty miles were a series of pools and portages. The pools were slow, and the portages were grueling: first the Sartell Dam, then on to Sauk Rapids, where racers had to portage around a whitewater stretch, and finally to the last portage at the St. Cloud Dam.

At each one, I had to load up all my gear—twenty pounds of water, two small coolers, and a dry bag—hoist up my canoe, then slog down the road. At the St. Cloud portage, a race volunteer sat in a chair, scrolling on his phone.

"Do you know how many miles are left?" I asked.

"Fifty miles."

"Are . . . you sure?" I asked.

"Let me check. Nope. Sorry, sixty miles."

"OK, thanks."

I lay in the grass for a few minutes and tried to sleep. But I'd consumed enough caffeine to paddle to New Orleans. So I just heaved my load, then started down the last portage. At the shore of the put-in, some kids were swimming below the dam.

"Nice kayak," one of them said.

"Thanks," I said. "It's actually a canoe."

"It's still nice."

Before getting back on the water, I took stock. I had a good supply of water and probably twice as much food as I needed. I figured I was still in last place. I was only half-paying attention during the safety meeting, so I didn't really know when the cutoff times were. And yet, for some reason, I felt a glimmer of hope. From here, the river was free-flowing—no more portages. If I was lucky, I would get to the finish in the early morning.

I pushed out into the river and had to cut straight across to make it through a rocky chute. Below the dam, the water was fast. I was rocketing along at seven miles an hour, my fastest pace yet. I felt good, and the sun was still high. Surely I could get to Coon Rapids. I was glad to be out here, on the river, watching it grow wider, becoming the Mississippi I knew.

After a few hours, the channel shifted east. The headwind was fierce, blowing at fifteen miles per hour, with thirty-mile-per-hour gusts. When the river turned south, I was sheltered. But whenever it turned east again, I got blasted by whitecaps and hit a wall of wind. The fastest I could move through these sections was two miles an hour. I could barely keep the canoe straight, and if I stopped paddling, I was blown back upstream.

Waves washed over the gunnels. I pushed through the eastern stretches with maddening torpor. I could feel my hopes of finishing begin to slip away.

It took three hours to cover the next ten miles, with a few tears and a lot of swearing. Night was falling when I dragged my canoe up onto a rocky shore. The temperature was dropping and would hit forty-six degrees that night. I was wet and shivering uncontrollably. I called my wife and promptly burst into tears. I told her I didn't think I was going to make it. She managed to talk me down, told me to put on some dry clothes, eat, and take a rest.

After we hung up, I felt better. I dug in my bag for a jacket and pants, which my fourteen-year-old daughter had goaded me into taking at the last minute. I didn't have a sleeping bag, but I did have an emergency bivouac—basically a heat blanket. So I crawled inside and lay in the grass shivering. I wondered idly: *What is medical attention? How does a person know if they need medical attention? Do I need medical attention? What would happen if I did need medical attention?*

The answer, I knew, was that I would lie here in the grass waiting for it. I thought of Benny Tonce and tried not to feel sorry for myself. I drifted off to sleep.

* * *

When I woke up an hour later, my body was warmer, but also damp from condensation. I watched the stars, which were beautiful and distant. I gauged the wind: still blowing, but not as hard. The air was cold, but I didn't want to lie in a wet plastic sack all night. So I climbed out, ate some food, drank some water, strapped everything in, and pushed out onto the river.

As soon as I did, I knew: this was a mistake. In the dim light, I could just make out the surface. But when the wind picked up, I couldn't tell the rocks from the shadows from the black water. Boulders came out of nowhere, looming out of the dark.

Why was I doing this? I tried to remember the reason. It seemed like it would be all too easy for me to find myself in the water, dragging my canoe to shore, then spending the rest of the night shivering onshore.

It was too late to turn back. The next place to land was about five miles downstream. If I just went slow and easy, and cautiously, I could be there in an hour and a half.

With my eyes glued to the water in front of me, I picked my way around the rocks. After a while, I started to relax. The night was peaceful and quiet. My wake was a silky gray line that cut through the water. A barred owl called. A pack of coyotes yipped in the night.

A few miles downstream, I came to the blinding lights of the Monticello nuclear power plant. Its floodlights were aimed down at the river, so the closer I got, the less I could see. I had no hope of spotting rocks ahead, so I just crossed my fingers and drifted downstream.

As I got closer to the plant, I could see more. There was a trail of foam on top of the water coming out of the plant. The air smelled strange.

On the left side of the channel was a sandbar with three people on it. At first I thought they were plant workers. But as I got closer, I could see they had a canoe, and they were setting up a tent. I later learned that these were MR150 racers who pulled over to warm up. After sleeping for about an hour, they were wakened by a booming amplified voice—like God—telling them the Department of Homeland Security had been notified, and they needed to leave.

Just around the corner from the plant, I came to a boat ramp. Another racer was already stopped there. I dragged my boat onshore and crawled into my heat blanket again to wait out the dark. As I drifted off to sleep, a meteor lit up the sky overhead.

Around 4:00 AM I woke up cold and wet again. There was a pink glow in the east. It was Sunday, and only thirty-three miles remained.

Daylight was a weaker tonic this time, but a tonic nonetheless. The end was in sight! It was time to go.

The day before, the field had spread out so much that I'd barely seen any other racers. The winning team, I would later learn, had finished in 23 hours and 33 minutes—about when I hit the halfway mark. A few others were close behind them, but nearly half the field had dropped out along the way.

Yet there were others who hung in for the second night, almost all of whom likewise hunkered down to escape the wind and cold. As day broke, they also got back on the water, and I started seeing other boats. A kayaker named Michael caught up to me and we paddled together for a few miles, commiserating about the cold, before he paddled on.

Mile by mile, the end got closer. The wind rose again, this time gusting up to nearly forty miles per hour. But it was mostly a tailwind, so at least it was pushing me home.

Before too long, there were twenty miles left.

Then fifteen.

Then ten.

Finally, I saw a concrete structure spanning the river: the Coon Rapids Dam. The end.

I was the twenty-sixth boat out of twenty-eight finishers (and forty-eight starters). And while there may not have been 100,000 people cheering as I pulled into the sheltered bay at the end of the race, a few people clapped when my boat touched the shore, then helped me stagger out of the water. It felt like a well-earned victory.

Over the next weeks, my thoughts kept returning to the river. At night, my dreams were all of paddling its bends and pools and little-known corners. I'd been part of the Mississippi's flow for only a few days, but the time went deep.

Because, as for all paddlers throughout time, the river, now more than it ever had, also flowed through me.

ADVENTURERS

THE SKY IS BURNING

Caught in the Pagami Creek Fire

BEFORE THEY EVEN SET THEIR KAYAKS IN THE WATER AT Kawishiwi Lake, Greg and Julie Welch had heard about the Pagami Creek Fire from the US Forest Service staffers who were watching it. They said it was small and hadn't moved much, and they had closed a swath of Minnesota's Boundary Waters Canoe Area that was twice as large as they thought necessary, just to be safe. The fire was about twenty miles to the west of the Welches' planned route.

Greg had been a photojournalist back in Michigan, where he often followed forest fire crews out to take photos. He had seen flames jump thirty-foot roadbeds and do other strange things. Given all he knew about fires, he figured they were more than a safe distance from it. Plus, the wind had been blowing the wrong way, gusting at their backs as they paddled north.

The day was perfect, seventy degrees, sunny, quiet—one of those days you dream of when you think about getting back into the wild. This was what they loved. This was what they looked forward to all year. During the summer, they worked twelve-hour days at their family business, building vinyl docks for people to put out behind their lake cabins. The orders came in an avalanche each spring, and they spent the rest of the summer digging out.

By August, things usually began to wind down, and they would pack their bags, strap their kayaks on the roof, leave their daughters (now fifteen and twenty years old) home with family, and head out for what Sigurd Olson once called "the singing wilderness." They had been doing this for the last twenty years. After two weeks cut off from everything but the calls of wolves and loons and eagles, they always came home feeling like new people.

This time, they planned to take it easy. By early afternoon, just two days into a ten-day trip, they reached Kawasachong Lake and found a campsite on the western side. It sat on top of a steep, twenty-five-foot bank, and it gave them a nice view of the water—calm and bright blue that day.

They beached their boats, hauled up their dry bags, and began the pleasant routine of setting up camp. After eating, they put up their tent, and Greg started getting ready to go fishing.

Around this time, the wind began to pick up, gusting. There seemed to be more smoke lingering around them. Far off, there was a strange cracking noise that sounded like branches breaking. Greg took a photo of the clouds to the west, and when he looked on the camera, there were streaks of orange shot through.

Julie was getting uneasy, so Greg agreed to paddle out and have a look to the west to see if the smoke from the Pagami Creek Fire looked any closer. He walked down to his kayak and paddled out into a little river just to the north of the lake.

As soon as he rounded a bend, he saw it: the entire horizon, all the way across, was on fire. The flames were horizontal, blowing straight at them.

* * *

The Pagami Creek Fire had started about three weeks earlier, when lightning stuck a bog east of Ely. It seemed to be slow moving and manageable. But on the day the Welches stopped at Kawasachong Lake, it became a fire of legend, racing across an unheard-of sixteen miles of land. It vaporized trees and resulted in a massive, 35,000-foot plume that created its own weather system. By the end of the day, the fire would consume some 92,000 total acres of wilderness.

Nothing in the historical record suggested that a fire could move that fast through the area. None of the alerts indicated conditions were even right for a fire of that scale. But a rare, unstable mass of air formed over the fire. At the same time, a strong wind kicked up out of the west, and the instability pulled it through the fire like a bellows blowing through a blacksmith's forge.

Greg raced back to the campsite as fast as he could, yelling up from the water for Julie to get moving. Julie had heard the fire roaring through the woods, though, and she was already throwing dry bags down to the shore before jumping herself.

Greg landed just as Julie got down, but she quickly realized she'd forgotten her life jacket, so Greg sprinted back up the bank. The smoke was so thick he had to grope around blindly inside the tent. He was already able to feel the heat from the fire, and his heart was racing. In the dark, he found two deflated air mattresses and grabbed them. Then his hand hit the life jacket; he snatched it and ran.

Julie was sitting in her kayak, watching her husband run to the shore. Just as he came down the slope, the fire crested over the bank and roared just a few feet behind him. Greg threw the life jacket to Julie and told her to go while he strapped the last bags onto his kayak and dragged it to the water.

The fire pushed a thick cloud of soot and ash ahead of it. As Julie paddled out, everything went black. She couldn't see Greg, so she screamed his name, but the fire roared like a freight train. All she could see was smoke and burning trees falling into the water. For a few seconds, she thought Greg was lost, and that she was too. She had no map, and no way to get back alone.

Then Greg appeared, paddling out of the smoke, a few feet away from her. But just as soon as she caught sight of him, the wind tossed her kayak into the air and flipped her into the cold water.

By the time she surfaced, the boat had been blown far across the lake. Greg paddled toward her, but the wind was too strong—he couldn't stop—and it blew him right past her. So he jumped in the water, holding his kayak and staying still, yelling for her to swim toward him. It took a few minutes for Julie to reach him, but together they clung to his boat while everything around them burned.

It was a world of black and orange. The islands in the lake were on fire. The entire shoreline was on fire. The air was thick with ash, soot, and glowing embers being blown across the lake at fifty miles an hour; they couldn't look west. Soot got in their eyes, coated their hair, their noses, and their throats. They had a fleece jacket, which they soaked in water to breathe through, but it didn't stop the headaches, the sense of being smothered, of drowning in air.

Everything was burning, and there was no place to go. They could duck their heads underwater for a few seconds to escape it all, but they couldn't keep doing that forever. They both were almost certain they were going to die, but after a brief talk, they agreed not to give up. Their daughters needed them.

So they treaded water, trying to stay in the middle of the lake, just waiting. After nearly an hour, Julie started to shiver uncontrollably, which Greg knew meant one thing: hypothermia. They were in danger of freezing to death while the world around them burned. They let the wind take them toward the eastern shore, where they could at least stand on the lake bottom. They drifted until they came to a boulder. They climbed on top and hauled the kayak out of the water too.

But before they could even begin to dry off, it started to rain. Not an ordinary rain, but a biblical, end-of-the-world kind of rain. It fell so hard that it hurt. Then, with a burst of thunder and lightning, the rain turned to hail. They held the deflated air mattresses above themselves for protection.

And then: nothing.

As suddenly as it had begun, the rain stopped. The fire died under the downpour. The sky cleared. High above them, the plume created by the Pagami Creek Fire had collapsed, sending all the moisture back down, extinguishing the flames, and, in the process, saving Greg and Julie Welch's lives.

But Julie was still shivering. Their tent was a pile of ashes, and the sun was sinking in the west, so there was not time to make their way back out. Sitting in the charred aftermath, the couple plotted their next move.

* * *

First they needed to find a place to camp. Miraculously, they located a small spot on a peninsula that had been spared from the fire.

Julie needed to warm up, but any wood that hadn't been burnt was soaked through with rain, so making a campfire was impossible.

They dug through the few dry bags that remained and found their camping stove, which they used for warmth. They ate what little food they had left and slept in a sleeping bag Greg found in another dry bag that had washed up onshore. As night set in, they lay in the sleeping bag together, wondering if the fire would return.

In the darkness around them, the shoreline glowed.

The next morning, they found Julie's kayak beached on some rocks across the lake. Then they paddled back down the stream that connected Kawasachong to another small, shallow body of water called Square Lake. Along the way, they watched for the bodies of a couple they'd passed the day before. If the others had camped anywhere along this creek, they wouldn't have made it, and the Welches would have to bear the grim news.

But they never came across any bodies. They made it to Square Lake, which had been completely burned as well, and then on to the sudden, strange greenness of Kawishiwi Lake, where their car was still parked, just as they'd left it. Back at the Forest Service district office in Tofte, where they stopped on their way out, they told their story to an incredulous forest ranger at the desk, who went to get his manager and make them tell it again.

From there, they drove on to Grand Marais, where they spent a few days unwinding, staring out across the water and trying to fathom what they'd just been through. They even drove up the Gunflint Trail and talked about camping at the end of it, then taking a day trip back into the Boundary Waters.

But it was all still too close, and the fear was too fresh. Besides, they would be back. The Boundary Waters always left them feeling a little more alive, and this time was no exception. So they packed their things, got in the car, and started the long drive back home to their daughters and their life.

Behind them, the memory of smoke and ash started to settle, while along the shores of Kawasachong Lake, new trees and brush would soon begin to grow.

NEVER SO TERRIFIED

A Night at Sturgeon Narrows

THE CAMPFIRE IS THE PERFECT PLACE FOR GHOST STORIES. But once in a while, the place you're camping *is* the story. In the lore of canoe country, one such place looms large: Sturgeon Narrows, a spit of land deep in Canada's Quetico Provincial Park.

I'd heard many stories about this place. In one, campers were almost struck by lightning as they arrived, then trees fell in a triangle around their tent that night. In another, Dan Liljedahl, a counselor at the YMCA's Camp Widjiwagan in northern Minnesota, arrived at Sturgeon Narrows with his campers. After dark, they heard a banging across the water, which turned out to be three canoes paddling toward their site. Dan's party waited for them to pass, but instead, the group stopped at Liljedahl's site, set up tents right next to the Widjiwagan group's, and barely said a word. Then they started a giant bonfire, Liljedahl wrote to me in an email, "like you have at the cabin getting rid of dead wood, and they start dancing and chanting . . . men and women. It all felt very ritualistic. The guys and I eventually fell into an uneasy sleep. I woke up early, got everyone up and we left."

But there is one story that haunts all who have heard it.

In 1972, when Attila Ray Dabasi was fourteen, he went on a seventeen-day canoe trip organized by Camp Widjiwagan. Dabasi, an artist in the Twin Cities, was a longtime Widjiwagan camper and counselor, and when I got in touch, he wrote up his account and sent it to me. His tentmate was Michael Phillips, thirteen, now a lawyer in Milwaukee and a former legal counsel for the Wisconsin Education Association Council. I called Phillips to ask him about the story. The two had not spoken since the 1970s, but he confirmed that Dabasi's version was essentially as he remembered it. All these years later, both of them are unsettled to think back on that night.

Here is the story of that night at Sturgeon Narrows, as told by Attila Ray Dabasi.

* * *

Many years ago, when I was a teenager, I had the good fortune to be introduced to a YMCA camp named Widjiwagan, based out of Ely, Minnesota, near the Boundary Waters Canoe Area. The camp specializes in wilderness canoe trips that introduce thirteen- to eighteen-year-olds to wilderness settings throughout Canada as well as the Boundary Waters.

This particular canoe trip was my second, and it took place in 1972, a few years before the Boundary Waters Canoe Area Wilderness was established. I went with four other teenagers and was led by a counselor who happened to be a University of Minnesota wrestler. We were out for seventeen days.

Our trip took place in Canada's Quetico Provincial Park, directly north of the BWCA. Canada's canoe country was more desolate, with less developed portages and campsites. It has lakes so big that you could spend a whole day paddling from one end to the other, especially if you were unfortunate enough to paddle into a wind.

For the first ten days of the trip, we were pelted with freezing rain. Even for Canada, such an unrelenting rain in July was highly unusual. Despite all of the obstacles and hardships, six of us city boys had managed to paddle and portage ourselves, with hundreds of pounds of food and equipment, over two hundred miles.

One thing that kept our momentum going was the goal of reaching the northernmost point of our trip. This was a lake described by others as the most beautiful and remote lake in the Quetico: Sturgeon Lake.

Sturgeon Lake had once been surrounded by ancient white pine. Those had been logged long ago by French Canadian lumberjacks and immigrants. The lake had several lumber camp ruins near its shores. The thought of rummaging through ruins fed our curiosity too, and compelled us to move on.

In the middle of the day we stopped for a bite to eat and studied the map for a campsite. Soon after we portaged into Sturgeon Lake, we spotted one right at the end of what looked like a river, a place named the Sturgeon Narrows.

As we paddled on to our evening's destination, we were rewarded with the sun breaking through the clouds. The rain subsided and a warm wind accompanied the sunlight.

The campsite was larger than most, with level ground, topsoil, and pine needles. We made camp late that afternoon, taking in the ambiance of what seemed like a perfect campsite. It faced south into the expanse of the lake. That evening, feeling the stress of the last ten days lift, we made a hearty Hudson Bay stew and hot chocolate.

For the first time in a long time, we were all content and getting along. At one point, I broke away from the group to do some exploring. I didn't go far from our base camp before I discovered the foundation of a structure. I also found some old rusty tin cans and the remnant of a rusty pitchfork with two bent tongs.

As I pondered the condition of the pitchfork, I had the overwhelming feeling I was being watched. My eyes darted around the area looking for signs of another being, but I concluded there was no one out there but me. Still, I felt uneasy enough to head back to the camp, where I found my buddies having a great time. After about an hour of raucousness, we began to settle down.

That night, my friend Michael and I were delegated to the two-man tent. The other tent was a spacious four-man tent, which we all preferred. We were taking turns sleeping in the smaller tent.

After turning in, we could hear the muffled conversations of our four companions some twenty feet away. After a while, a chorus of snoring emerged from their tent, which in turn gave us the confidence to diss one of the guys in that tent, named Scott.

He was a loud, obnoxious guy, who was fortunately more funny than annoying. He helped provide comic relief on days of the trip when the going got rough. When Michael and I were sure Scott was asleep, we started exchanging anecdotes about him, each more hilarious than the last. The stories peaked with Michael and me in a fit of hysterics.

Our laughter abruptly ended when we heard a single deafening THUD from the forest. In the light from the partial moon, I could see the look on Michael's face: "WHAT THE HELL WAS THAT?"

I felt a wave of terror wash over my body. We lay in the tent frozen by fear, completely tuned in to sounds outside our thin-walled shelter.

Then there was another THUD.

And another.

And another.

I looked at Michael's face, and his expression turned from fear to a smile.

"Ha, ha, ha, Scott!" he said. "Like that's going to scare us." Then he added in a sarcastic tone, "You're so cool man! Sooo cool! Ha, ha, ha."

Scott did not respond.

The thudding continued, growing in its intensity and resonance, vibrating the ground all the way to our tent. The ground was shaking so violently that it felt like the trees around our campsite were falling over one by one. It sounded like some giant force was tearing them out of the ground, roots and all.

What really caused me to panic, though, was the sound of the birds going berserk. Birds of all types, waked by the commotion, were screeching and flapping their wings as they tried to flee the area.

Michael and I crammed ourselves into the very center of our tent. The chaos around us reached deafening proportions. It was an overwhelming sound, like standing next to an enormous waterfall. Neither one of us said a word. It was understood we weren't being pranked by Scott. The force of what was happening outside our tent was well beyond anything a person could produce in the middle of nowhere.

To this day, I have never been so terrified in my life. My head flooded with the idea of death. In my delirious state of mind, I started a conversation with God. I asked him to forgive me for all the people I may have hurt up until that point of my short fourteen years of life. Another thought I had was that I hadn't even kissed my first girl yet. But the most painful image was of my mother receiving news of my grisly death.

Then, without warning, it stopped. Silence. The night air was empty of all sounds, not even the wind.

With our full attention focused on the quiet, we turned to each other. In whispering voices, we weighed the idea of making a run for it to where our buddies and the college wrestler were. Besides, they must have been awake with the horror show playing out around us.

Then we heard something else. From the waters south of our campsite, voices burst into laughter and song. The clarity of those voices was so sharp that I could hear they were having a great time.

As I listened, I also realized that the speaking and singing were all in French. And they were getting louder. Whomever the voices belonged to were paddling some kind of boat toward our campsite.

It didn't take long for them to arrive. Raucous laughter ensued as they landed. We listened for footsteps, but instead we heard the clanging of the pots and pans we'd placed on our food packs as a bear alarm. Next we heard our food packs and our personal packs being ripped apart and shredded.

We lay there too frightened to move, until a voice came from our buddies' tent, blurted through the noise. With that single sound, the chaos stopped. Michael and I assessed the situation, wondering if it was time to make a run for the other tent.

I yelled: "Jim, are you awake, man?"

No response.

We exploded out of our tent and ran to where our companions were. As we did, Michael shined his flashlight around us, looking for whatever had terrified us. The beam managed to penetrate about six feet of the darkness, keeping us blind to whatever it was.

In a single motion, we unzipped the tent and dove into safety, landing on four very asleep guys who suddenly found themselves abruptly woken by two frantic kids. The voice we'd heard just moments before had been one of them talking in his sleep. I landed on the wrestler, whose face I unintentionally bounced into the ground.

Punching, kicking, and threats ensued, with all four guys wide awake and enraged. They didn't believe a word we said, and they threw us out of their tent.

Outside, Michael and I stood for a minute trying to see anything we could with his flashlight. But there was nothing. We slowly walked back to our tent, then we stood for a bit, listening, before we climbed back in.

In the tent, we talked about what had happened, trying to explain it or rationalize it. Soon Michael dozed off with a slight snore. I lay motionless, my ears tuned to our surroundings.

After some time, in the far distance, the thumping returned. It was a little slower with each stomp. As I listened, it took on a soothing quality, and soon I was asleep.

The next morning, we woke up to four really angry guys, including our counselor, who had a freshly cut lip. As for the campsite, there was no evidence of any damage. Everything, including the trees around us, looked just as we left it the night before. Michael and I tried to explain the events of that evening, but we were met with disbelief, anger, and, eventually, deaf ears. No one believed our story.

Later that day, as we paddled away from our campsite, I felt the sweet rush of mad relief that comes with a narrow escape. I knew we were free of that place and was thankful never to return.

It was a perfect, windless summer morning. The water was as smooth as a sheet of ice. As we crossed the lake, one of the guys yelled, "What the fuck is that?"

We all turned to look back. A single, tall birch tree surrounded by shrubs—with something rustling within their leaves—was swaying back and forth.

Everything else stood silent and still on that perfect summer morning.

THE CALL OF THE RIVER

IN THE SUMMER OF 2012, DEVIN BROWN FLEW FROM NEW York City to Minneapolis to help remodel the Apple Store in the Southdale Mall. Brown was a "visual specialist" from the Apple Store in Grand Central Station—a coveted position, occupied by just a handful of people across the country. Below her as she flew in was a ribbon of water that wound through the city and would soon wind through her life: the Mississippi River.

When Brown landed, her great-aunt Gwen Leeds, who had moved to Minnesota in the 1980s, picked her up. Gwen's husband, Alan, had come to Minnesota to work as Prince's road manager, and Gwen also ended up working for the Purple One.

A few days later, Brown drove to work in Edina. On the way, she stopped at Lake Harriet, rented a kayak, and paddled around. "What I loved about Minnesota was how you could leave work, hop on a lake, then get home in time for dinner," Brown says. "On the East Coast, you're in traffic for forever to get outdoors."

Brown's aunt also took her to Nicollet Island, where they stood under the Hennepin Avenue Bridge watching the Aquatennial fireworks. As impressive as the sky was that night, it was the river that made a deeper impression. "I remember how calming, but also exciting and powerful, the energy that came off the river was," she says. "It was compelling. I was intrigued. I wanted to learn more about it."

* * *

Brown grew up in Glen Ridge, New Jersey, a mostly white commuter suburb outside New York City. At the time, she didn't know why all the Black and poor kids, including herself, were the only ones in special education classes (she's dyslexic), or why she was excluded from certain social functions, or why, in college, her first roommate tried to get her kicked out of the dorm by saying she was "dirty."

"I've always been the only Black person, or Black female, in all-white spaces," Brown says. "When you grow up like that, you don't necessarily notice the microaggressions, because they're just so normal and ingrained. But I've always just been a survivor. I've had to fight for everything I've gotten."

After leaving Minneapolis, Brown went back to her 5:30 AM commute, her sky-high cost of living, and her stressful workplace. She felt burned out and had developed a limp her doctors couldn't explain.

Most of all, she missed the outdoors. As a toddler, Brown had gone to a summer camp run by her aunt. Often, her family went car camping at a state campground, where she learned to swim. And as soon as she was old enough, she went to camp at Frost Valley YMCA in the Catskill Mountains every summer, where she later worked as an adventure trip leader.

By the spring of 2013, Brown had had enough. She gave notice at Apple and went back to work at Frost Valley for the summer. Two days after she arrived, her limp went away.

Soon she started making bigger plans. She would move to Minnesota, and she would paddle the entire length of the Mississippi River, from source to sea.

"Devin really leans into what calls her," says her friend Jeanette Fordyce. "So many people get in their own way, overthinking. But Devin is like 'Nope. This is what it's going to be.'"

Brown's college classmate Alyssa Mollica attended her going-away party.

"Devin is incredibly inspirational," Mollica says. "She's tough, because she's had to be. She's incredibly kind. And she's always done what she wanted to do, unapologetically. I remember meeting her in a poetry class on Robert Frost and thinking, *My god, she's got it together at eighteen*. I was just floored."

In February of 2014, after cashing out her 401(k) and stock options, Brown landed in Minneapolis as a polar vortex was whipping across the state. Slowly, she started building her new life. She had lined up one summer job leading kayaking tours on the Mississippi, but when the owner saw her, he gave her an office job instead. Later, a fellow worker confided that the owner had said she didn't "look like a kayaker." She sent her letter of resignation.

Instead, she got a job at Midwest Mountaineering during the week. On weekends, she took the Northstar train line to Clearwater to work as a software consultant at Clear Waters Outfitting on the Mississippi River. Each evening she paddled upstream to an island, where she set up her tent for the night. In the morning, she paddled back down to work.

"It was awesome," Brown says. "At night, I could see the raccoon eyes, but they stayed away because I had a fire. It was an awesome summer."

* * *

Summer ended. Brown kept working at Midwest Mountaineering and did other odd jobs to make ends meet, but it wasn't enough. With her savings dwindling, she started looking for a viable career path.

One day after her bus ticket home expired, she walked past the Aveda Institute, where she saw an ad for its massage school. She said to herself: *Massage therapy. I'd be good at that.* She took the first available tour, enrolled on the spot, and started classes four days later.

Meanwhile, a lot of life happened. Brown became a single mom to a son. Her grandmother, with whom she was extremely close, passed away. And her mother moved to Minneapolis to be with her new grandchild.

"She called me," says Leslie Brown, "and said, 'If you want to be in your grandchild's life, I suggest you pack your stuff, because I'm not coming back.' So I gave my job notice, packed up, put all my stuff in storage, and I came on out here."

Slowly, things came together, and Brown's dream of paddling down the Mississippi remained at the center. "I had these goals I needed to put in place to build toward it," she says. "Like: I need to buy a house so I can store the boat. And I need to buy a car that can carry the boat. And finally I got the house, and I got the car, and I got the boat. Now I just have to get the money to make it down the river."

She also got more involved in the community, connecting people of color—especially young people—with the river. As program manager at Mississippi Park Connection, a partnership with the National Park Service, Brown led Black, Indigenous, and people of color (BIPOC) affinity group paddles. "Devin's welcoming presence on the Mississippi River is infectious," says Mississippi Park Connection assistant director Anna Waugh. "She is opening doors to hundreds of new paddlers across the Twin Cities and helping diverse audiences to fall in love with the Mississippi River. We've been able to serve way more people than in past years, thanks to Devin."

Brown also works with the community youth organization Intentions and its Environmentally Conscious Youth program. "We're partnering with Devin to help get youth out into nature, do cleanups, and to spread the word about protecting our natural resources," says executive director Yaya Cochran. "She's someone young people really look up to. Every time we have kids around, they gravitate to her."

* * *

One day in November, I meet Brown at Boom Island Park in Northeast Minneapolis. We put on our dry suits, set our boats in the Mississippi, and paddle upstream.

The last time I'd seen Brown with her kayak was at the start of the MR150, a 150-mile canoe race on the Mississippi we both entered. But I hadn't seen her for long. She had taken off like a shot and was soon out of sight, while I'd languished around last place.

Today Brown slows down for me as we chat about the race. She dropped out around mile seventy, she tells me, for many reasons: The water was extremely low. She hadn't been able to train much because her car was in the shop from an accident, which had also hurt her back. She had used all her fresh clothes and was badly chilled.

Yet there was another factor, one that she alone had to face. After the first portage, Brown saw a group of men in a backyard on the river. Just as she was thinking how nice it would be to have a home on the Mississippi, one of them looked over and yelled a racial slur.

The word landed like a bomb. Brown had never been called the N-word to her face. It shattered her peace of mind. It destroyed her sense of safety. She found another racer to paddle with for a while, which helped. She worked to pull herself together, but when darkness fell, she worried about going ashore.

"It definitely messed with her head," says her friend Fordyce. "The river is Devin's safe space, her place of grounding. And that was stripped of her. It's just such a reality, how dangerous accessing the outdoors can be for people of color. She's doing her part to make Black people feel comfortable out on the water, and to make herself feel safe. But she can only protect herself so much. It's white people's work to figure out how to not have that happen again. We all need to do a lot of work around that."

On the river north of Boom Island, Brown and I paddle on. When I ask what scares her most about her upcoming Mississippi trip, she doesn't hesitate. "Racists," she says. "The most dangerous thing on the trail is always other people."

With that in mind, Brown has refocused her Mississippi journey more as a community event than a solo one, and she is working to find people who want to paddle sections with her. Because even though there might be dangers—human and otherwise—she's going, unapologetically.

We move north on the river, past an abandoned railroad bridge where, the week before, a bunch of kids stood yelling, "Is that Devin? That's Devin!" It turned out to be a group she'd taken paddling a month earlier.

Further north, we come to a small island with a heron rookery in its trees. At this time of year, the nests are empty. "How many nests do you think there are?" I ask.

"Maybe a hundred," she says.

"Have you ever seen it when it's full of babies?" I ask.

"Yeah," Brown says. "The energy of the island is very different."

"They're such cranky birds," I say. "Most of the time they don't like each other, but then they come together here."

She looks up from the river, into the trees full of nests.

"Well," she says, "there are things we do for survival."

The RACE *for the* RECORD

FOR THE RECORD(S)

An Author's Note

IN 2019, I GOT AN ASSIGNMENT FOR *OUTSIDE* MAGAZINE TO write about KJ Millhone's 2020 Mississippi River paddling record. This attempt was canceled due to the pandemic, as was my assignment. But in 2021, both were revived with the dueling attempts of Millhone and Scott Miller. "An Epic Battle" is the reported version of those two attempts.

During that time, I also volunteered as a support crew member for Millhone's team, while writing (fairly, I hope) about both attempts. My original draft of the story had third- and first-person elements—my view from the crew. But these crewing sections were rightly cut to leave just the third-person version.

"Crewing the Record" is made up of those sections that were cut, and stands as a behind-the-scenes look at the high-stress, high-stakes enterprise that is crewing a Mississippi River paddling record. The events take place simultaneously with "An Epic Battle," from April to May of 2021.

Two years later, in May of 2023, I also served on the support crew for Scott Miller's record attempt, though only through Minnesota. I didn't see enough of the attempt to write a full crewing account, but the chapter "A Race for Redemption" takes place in that context, and with that access and point of view.

For a look at these attempts in the larger context, please see Appendix A.

AN EPIC BATTLE

AROUND 4:00 AM ON MAY 5, 2021, ON THE MISSISSIPPI RIVER north of Memphis, Tennessee, Bobby Johnson was sitting in the bow of a four-person canoe, peering into the night. In front of him, through the dark, he could make out a wing dam, one of the underwater structures used by the US Army Corps of Engineers to push water into the main channel.

Most boats can't pass over wing dams without losing a propeller or a motor, but a canoe can usually glide by without a scrape. As the boat crossed it, though, Johnson noticed a pull to the right.

For a second, he wondered why Casey Millhone, the twenty-year-old in the stern who was taking a semester off from Colorado College, had ruddered that way. He quickly realized she hadn't: a massive whirlpool was drawing them in.

Johnson, a lanky forty-three-year-old car dealer from Florida, was one of four people in the Wenonah canoe trying to break the record for paddling the Mississippi River from end to end, set in 2003. That year, canoeing icon Bob Bradford and his partner, Clark Eid, had raced down all 2,350 miles in just over eighteen days.

Johnson's team was helmed by sixty-two-year-old KJ Millhone—Casey's father, who in 1980 set the Mississippi paddling record at thirty-five days. The elder Millhone called the new crew "Mile Marker Zero," after the channel marker south of New Orleans that demarcates the official end of the river. The group was rounded out by a barrel-chested sixty-one-year-old named Rod Price, also from Florida.

Both older men were asleep when their craft approached the swirling hole in the river. The canoe went straight in, riding down it like a hill. The bow plunged through the far side of the whirlpool, and Johnson was submerged up to his neck. Fortunately, the spray skirt across his lap kept enough water out that he popped up on the other side.

The stern naturally followed Johnson down into the vortex, then up the other side. When the canoe exited, it spun. Casey screamed as it tipped, then—mimicking a sailing move called *hiking*—she stood and leaned out to the side, over the water, to keep the boat afloat.

It worked. The two sleeping team members woke up in half a foot of freezing water, shivering and disoriented. But the vessel righted itself.

Meanwhile, a thousand river miles to the north, a pursuit was underway. The day before, when the sun rose, another team of four paddlers walked their canoe down to the Mississippi River's headwaters in northern Minnesota's Lake Itasca. Team "Mississippi Speed Record" was helmed by Scott Miller, a bearded, forty-five-year-old oncology nurse and onetime Eagle Scout from Minneapolis.

The year before, Miller and Millhone had been teammates, working together to break the record. Then, just as they were about to set off, the team fractured, turning their joint attempt into a bitter race.

By the time Miller and his team launched, KJ Millhone and his crew were almost halfway down the Mississippi. This could have been a disadvantage—at the headwaters, the river levels were lower and the water was slow. But there was an upside: by watching Mile Marker Zero's progress, which was publicly available on Garmin's live tracking website and on the real-time boat-racing site RaceOwl, they could see their rivals' times at each checkpoint, so they knew exactly how fast they needed to go to win.

* * *

In the 1970s, a boy in Minnesota was leafing through the *Guinness Book of World Records*, dreaming about which ones might be broken. KJ Millhone considered the number of grapes eaten in a minute, which seemed impossible when he put them on a scale. He started training for the rope-jumping record, but gave up after losing several toenails.

The Mississippi River, on the other hand, was like a math problem: Millhone figured he could paddle at least fifty miles a day, getting him within range of the 1937 record of forty-nine days.

In 1978, a British Royal Air Force team of six, paddling tandem kayaks, trimmed that record to forty-two days, but Millhone was undeterred. The next year, he started planning an attempt with a friend named Steve Eckelkamp.

In August of 1980, the two put in at Lake Itasca. Supported by a two-man crew, they paddled for 35 days, 11 hours, and 27 minutes before reaching the end and beating the RAF team by seven days.

The record dropped a little here and there over the ensuing decades, until 2003, when Bradford and Eid, canoeing through lightning storms and high winds that sent trees flying across the river—and sleeping just four hours a day—made it in an astounding 18 days, 4 hours, and 51 minutes, setting a nearly impossible standard.

* * *

Eckelkamp was mowing his lawn in 2017 when he had a massive heart attack and died at age sixty. Millhone flew to Nashville, Tennessee, to speak at his funeral, where he shared stories about their Mississippi record, an aborted trip down the Amazon, and a paddle up Canada's Pacific coast.

Hearing these wild tales, Eckelkamp's nephew, Kevin, decided he wanted to take on the Mississippi record himself. So he and a friend, Nate Lastinger, both living in Florida, bought a canoe and started training.

They called Millhone to ask for advice. The older man dug out his boxes of photos and papers from the trip. He also found a note that he and Eckelkamp had jotted down on the ride back from Mile Marker Zero: it was a plan for how the river could be run in as few as fifteen days, using on-the-water support, which no one had yet tried.

As Millhone began looking through the mementos, the juices started flowing, and he went to Florida to teach the youngsters how to paddle. He says they asked him to be on their team. Lastinger says it was the other way around. Either way, they launched an attempt together in May of 2018.

By the time they got to Iowa, however, they were down to two paddlers—Lastinger dropped out because his son needed surgery—and they were 13.5 hours behind pace. That was when Millhone pulled the plug. "I didn't want to stop," he says, "but I also thought, *I'm not in this for fun. I'm in this to get the record.*"

* * *

Back home, near Lake Minnetonka, outside Minneapolis, Millhone considered making another attempt. Having lasted more than seven hundred miles, he realized he might just be able to paddle the whole river again. Then, one night at dinner, during a discussion about it, Casey turned to her father.

"Dad," she said, "if you're going to do this, I want to be part of it."

For Millhone, that settled it. The race for the record was on. "How can a father turn down the opportunity to try this kind of thing with his only child?" Millhone asked.

Soon after that, Scott Miller, who had seen an article about the 2018 attempt, reached out to Millhone on Facebook. In 2005, on the seventy-fifth anniversary of Eric Sevareid's 1930 *Canoeing with the Cree* expedition, Miller and a friend had paddled some two thousand miles from Minnesota to Hudson Bay. He wanted to know if Millhone was planning another Mississippi attempt.

The two met. They talked. They paddled. They bought a boat. They made a plan. They interviewed other paddlers and signed up a Wisconsin kayak guide named Oliver Simes.

The four trained throughout the summer of 2019. They installed a rudder in their twenty-three-foot, Wenonah Minnesota 4 Kevlar canoe and built a modified sleeping compartment, so two people could paddle in the bow and stern while two others kept dry and slept in the middle. They went on training trips, and on each, they performed as good as or better than the record pace.

By early 2020, they were ready for an April launch, but in March, the pandemic hit. Minnesota governor Tim Walz put the state in lockdown and issued a stay-at-home order. The water was fast and high. The weather looked good. As the departure date loomed, the team discussed what to do. Millhone wanted to go and thought it could be done safely. Miller wasn't sure. Millhone gave him two weeks to decide.

"If you back out after you make this decision," Millhone told him, "we're over."

Miller agreed to go. But as soon as he hung up the phone, regret rushed in. A few days later, he called to say he was out for 2020 but would go in 2021. "I just had a stone in my gut," says Miller. "I'm a nurse and a citizen of this country. We had this terrifying pandemic that no one knew anything about. I wasn't going to break the stay-at-home orders. It seemed like an unpatriotic thing to do."

Millhone was on his way back from Utah with a support boat, a well-used pontoon he had bought for the trip, when he received the call. He was ready. He was sixty-one, and his window of opportunity wouldn't stay open forever. He'd already endured one round of back surgery so he could do the trip, and he thought this might be his last shot. He was livid, and he accused Miller of betrayal. Miller said Millhone wasn't being a friend. Then Simes bowed out as well.

They divided up the team assets. Miller took most of the support crew with him, including crew chief Moose Dougherty, who was his wife's uncle. Millhone wanted to keep the equipment because he still hoped to find replacement paddlers for 2020. When none emerged, he resigned himself to a 2021 launch. After he'd cooled off, he called Miller to ask him back on the team.

Miller declined. "I was like, that ship has sailed," he says. "You burned this bridge really hard."

The team was done.

* * *

Summer came. Millhone and Miller each regrouped and tried to decide how to proceed. They each needed paddlers, so they began to search within the niche world of competitive canoeing.

Millhone managed to sign up Rod Price, a Florida canoeist who had won more than three hundred paddling races, including the Yukon 1000, and Bobby Johnson, also from Florida, who in a few years of racing had already become something of a legend. In the 2019 Alabama 650, with just forty miles to go, Johnson came from twenty miles behind to win. Millhone's daughter Casey was the fourth.

Miller, for his part, secured a fifty-nine-year-old kayaker from St. Louis named Perry Whitaker, who had finished the Missouri 340 several times. He also signed up Joel Ford, thirty-six, who was on the United States Adventure Racing Association's 2018 national championship team, and Adam Macht, thirty-four, a tall, powerful paddler from northern Minnesota who regularly put in fifty-plus-mile days through the Boundary Waters. And he bought a Wenonah Minnesota 4 canoe.

Both teams trained through the winter. By the spring of 2021, they felt confident and ready. Millhone had world-class paddlers, but weaker support on the water: an aging pontoon, modified for the attempt, with just four people to run it.

Miller's support included three boats and a large crew that had worked with the team on at least five practice trips. His group even had two portable toilets to make bathroom breaks as efficient as possible.

"I'd like to think my team can match them speed-wise, and hopefully even be faster," said Miller. "But even if we can't match them on speed, our organization, our teamwork, our planning, our support crew, and our quick transitions—that's where I'm hoping to get the edge."

Millhone was out for blood. "I don't really care whether we start at the same time, we chase them down, or they're behind us," he said. "I just want to kick their asses."

* * *

On April 22, 2021, Millhone and his team walked their boat down to Lake Itasca's rocky spillway, where the Mississippi begins. The sun was bright. The lake was like glass. A river of possibilities stretched out in front of them.

At 8:00 AM, they set their boat in the frigid, clear water and were off.

The team moved slowly at first, behind Bradford and Eid's 2003 record pace. Then Millhone came down with a flu-like illness. For the first twenty-four hours, he was unable to keep any food down and became badly dehydrated. At the edge of Lake Winnibigoshish, a sixteen-mile-wide body of water on the river's northern stretch, the team's doctor hooked him up to an IV, and he lay in the RV for two and a half hours recovering.

That night they paddled through a whiteout blizzard, thick snow blocking their view of the tree-lined banks. The next day the snow turned into a cold, endless rain. It was not the initial push they'd hoped for. But as the river widened and grew, they picked up speed. By the time they hit Minneapolis on day four, they were ten hours ahead of the 2003 record pace.

South of the city, the team met its support boat, an over-engineered death trap with a heavy canoe cradle mounted on one side. In theory, the pontoon boat would anchor and the canoe would slide into the cradle, so the paddlers could be resupplied without having to go ashore. In practice, the thing could barely float because it was so heavily loaded with freezers, a microwave, a generator, and other gear—and its pontoons leaked. On the first night, the boat nearly sank on Lake Pepin as its crew tried to anchor. The next morning, the team discovered that two of the three pontoons were full of water.

Leaving the support boat behind the morning of day five, the paddlers raced on through Minnesota and Wisconsin, while the support crew—complete with cooks, the doctor, and a social media coordinator, and led by KJ's wife, Lisa Millhone—scrambled to find landings to meet them. In the canoe, the team tried to adapt to the schedule. Each of them would sleep for three hours, then paddle for nine.

To pass the time, KJ told stories about his trip down the river in 1980. Johnson joked, sang, and dispensed relationship advice. Price reminisced about growing up in Florida and kept tabs on their pace. Casey, using an iPad mounted on a thwart, navigated and tried to keep them in the main channel.

Their lead grew. One night they were caught in a thunderstorm so violent that a lockmaster nearly didn't let them pass, claiming it was too dangerous.

By the time the pontoons were repaired and the support crew returned to the water, night was falling on day six. The team was well into Iowa and twelve hours ahead of pace. The four members were a machine, racing around the clock.

Then, during the first night back on the water, the support boat crashed into a buoy, lost its depth finder, and nearly sank again while trying to anchor. The following morning, when the pontoon limped into the small tourist town of Savanna, Illinois, it was listing badly, and the right pontoon was full of water again. The vessel was done.

Fortunately, the team was nearly seventeen hours ahead of pace. As the canoe made its way south, Johnson carried on a debate about whether it would be better to drive a train or pilot a barge. At night Casey tried to navigate conversations with her hallucinating father, who held imaginary dialogues with Richard Nixon and who jumped in his seat when he mistook a tree on the bank for Sasquatch.

With the loss of the support boat, the team's lead started to slip: first to fifteen hours, then thirteen, then eleven. Johnson kept suggesting they switch to four paddlers to gain time, instead of three people paddling with one sleeping. But when Price suggested they switch during Johnson's sleep shift, he dropped it.

By the time they got to St. Louis, with more than eleven hundred miles to go, their lead was down to nine hours. One problem: when team Mile Marker Zero stopped, it *stopped*—sometimes for nearly an hour. The paddlers sat in chairs and got massages. They ate pizza and talked. KJ looked exhausted and wandered around like a zombie. Johnson was usually pissed about not being able to find something he wanted. Price would complain about the lack of efficiency, then crawl into the RV and fall asleep. Casey spent a lot of time huddled in conversation with her mom. Whenever they pulled off the river, it felt more like an exhausted beach party than a NASCAR pit stop.

South of St. Louis, the support crew finally launched a brand-new pontoon, which they had bought in Iowa. Late that night, the team reached Cairo, Illinois, where the Ohio River pours into the Mississippi. The area was industrial and thick with barge traffic.

A storm rolled in, tearing trees into splinters up and down the river, and the National Weather Service advised everyone to take shelter on the first floor of their home. The canoe and the new support boat barely made it to an island, where they remained pinned down until the tempest passed.

The next morning, their lead was down to seven hours.

* * *

A thousand miles upstream on that same morning, on Tuesday, May 4, Miller and his team launched. Millhone was chasing history. Now Miller was chasing him.

Things didn't start well for team Mississippi Speed Record either. The later launch meant the water levels were lower, and the paddlers' pace was even slower through the shallows and swamps. When they reached Knutson Dam, in the dense pines of Minnesota's Chippewa National Forest, they were already two hours behind Mile Marker Zero's pace and four hours behind the record. As the boat moved south, the gap widened.

Miller's team, as he predicted, wasn't quite as fast on the water. But off it, they moved with military efficiency—their stops lasted around ten minutes, with only four or five stops each day. And yet they were losing time and couldn't figure out why, until Ford, drawing on his adventure-racing experience, concluded that with two sleep shifts of three hours each, they weren't getting enough rest. So they threw out the old schedule and made a new one.

Now instead of three people paddling at night, they would have two, while the others slept for four hours. At 2:00 AM, they would switch. During the day, between 6:00 AM and 10:00 PM, they kept three paddles in the water and they each got another four-hour sleep shift, for a total of eight hours.

With this new routine, everyone got more rest. They felt better. They pushed harder. At night they moved faster, energized by two fresh paddlers instead of three exhausted ones. The game had changed.

* * *

By day fourteen, Mile Marker Zero was nearing the finish, but the river was taking its toll. With the new support boat on the water and a huge push from an Ohio River raging from the rain, they should have been racking up time. But they weren't. Instead, the record was slipping away. Two days after the big storm south of Cairo, and one day after the giant whirlpool, the team's lead was less than four and a half hours.

Speed was not a problem. The paddlers were hitting ten and eleven miles per hour at times. But they were still stopping every three hours to change positions, which meant eight breaks a day. Price told Johnson they needed to stop the bleeding, so they started policing their changes more aggressively. They paddled harder.

Then they got a break: near Greenville, Mississippi, just north of the Louisiana border, the harsh spring weather changed. It stopped raining. The wind calmed. The support boat found its rhythm. Their transitions quickened. They moved faster, hitting average speeds of seven and eight miles per hour, covering as much as 180 miles a day.

When they reached Baton Rouge, Louisiana, two days later—weaving between barges and oceangoing ships—their lead over the record was back up to nine hours.

* * *

Mississippi Speed Record, however, was clawing back time with its new strategy. When they hit Alton, Illinois, flying past the limestone cliffs north of town, they were only ten minutes behind the pace of Mile Marker Zero. By the time the boat went around the next bend, at the mouth of the Missouri River, the team was thirty minutes ahead.

Things were looking up for Miller, and he and his paddlers were having a great time. Multiple times a day, Adam Macht would burst into refrains from Dolly Parton's "Islands in the Stream." Once a barge captain called over the radio, saying, "Y'all better get to a side, because I've got you lined up in my jack staff," meaning the flagpole on the front of the boat. Over the noise of the river, however, they heard it as "jackstache," and soon this new term for whatever lay in front of them peppered their conversations.

Currently in their jackstache was one of the most dangerous parts of the Mississippi: a jagged row of boulders, where the river drops roughly ten feet, called the Chain of Rocks. The only way to get past the section is to shoot through a small slot in the middle. The way around it is a diversion channel, a narrow stretch of water that runs parallel to the main river. Millhone and his team had taken the canal, which cost them several hours as they waited for barges to lock through.

Miller's team spent a tense hour debating whether to risk the faster route. In the end they decided to go for it, figuring they had about a 70 percent chance of making it. They had three support boats on the water, so they were able to unload all their gear upstream and have another boat waiting below, in case they dumped.

As they approached the chain, fans stood on the bridge overhead, cheering and ringing bells, while some seven hundred people watched on Facebook Live. The rocks loomed just below the surface. Over the din, Perry Whitaker shouted, "It's too late to turn back now, motherfuckers!"

They paddled hard toward a narrow V; water sprayed up as they shot through. The bow careered over the drop, tipping forward and down, before leveling out on the water below. They were on the other side, and their lead over Millhone had jumped to two hours.

* * *

For Mile Marker Zero, the end was in sight. In New Orleans they cruised past the French Quarter, where the previous night's vomit was still being sprayed off Bourbon Street.

The river was packed with traffic: cargo ships, navy vessels, heavy barges, and the tugs that pushed them. The team maneuvered around these obstacles as best it could, while the support crew talked to ship captains on the marine radio. With less than a hundred miles to go, the record seemed to be in the bag.

Just south of the city, the new support boat was approaching shore to anchor for a shift change when the crew heard a loud scraping. The vessel stopped moving; it was hung up on a rock. The pilot gunned the motor, and there was another loud sound as the propeller sheared off.

For the third time, the support boat was down, so the paddlers took whatever supplies they could gather and set off down the last stretch of river. Millhone recognized the danger: night was falling; weather forecasters said a huge thunderstorm was coming, and there were ships everywhere.

Fortunately, the team had been in touch with a river pilot named Joey Cargol, who had canoed the entire Mississippi himself in 2020. He offered to use his boat to help guide them through the treacherous waters at the river's end. Cargol took aboard a few support crew members, and they found a boat landing around Mile Marker 30 where they could launch. They sped upstream to meet the canoe, to the paddlers' great relief.

When the team arrived at Mile Marker 25, they unloaded everything they could onto Cargol's boat. They also installed a fourth seat in the canoe, so all four could paddle to the end. This move likely saved their lives.

The area where the Mississippi empties into the Gulf of Mexico is full of so-called passes, channels that run sideways from the main river, through bayous, and out to the Gulf. Around the next bend, they came to a series of such channels, over a mile long, known as Mardi Gras Pass, where the water near the east bank spills over a one-foot drop into a channel that leads away from the river. Cargol knew this was an extremely dangerous spot: almost every year, a duck hunter got sucked over the spillway and drowned. The drop-off was hard to see in the dark, but as they rounded the corner, Cargol sensed they were too close. Then, to his horror, he watched as the canoe slipped down through the whitewater, pulled off the river into the pass's channels. His heart sank. *There is no way they're getting out of there*, he thought.

But the paddlers knew what to do. They were in sync, and after nearly tipping once, they turned the canoe around and started pushing back toward the river with everything they had.

Cargol watched in shock as the team paddled back up the drop-off. “They just hit a gear that I’ve never seen anyone hit,” he said afterward. “They powered back into the river against, easily, an eight- to ten-knot current [nine to eleven miles per hour]. I don’t know how they did it.”

Back in the river, the team continued downstream. Then, half a mile later, they met a north- and southbound ship at the same point. The ships raised the water level and pushed the canoe back over the drop into another channel of Mardi Gras.

One more time, they powered back up. This time, they hit rocks, had to slide the canoe back down into the pass, and then paddled the boat back up into the main channel again.

Just before 4:00 AM, the team came into an area known as the Head of Passes, where the river splits into three channels. The place was filled with brightly lit ships, dredges, and channel markers. Casey pointed them toward Mile Marker Zero, and they went for it. Cargol radioed a ship captain to shine his spotlight on the small wood and metal tower that is the marker.

At 3:52 AM, they arrived. The current was so strong that it was hard to keep their position, but Casey and Johnson climbed up the tower and cheered while Price and KJ stayed in the canoe and held on to the structure.

Forty years earlier, when Millhone reached Mile Marker Zero, he threw up his paddle and embraced his friend, and they tipped the canoe over in their celebration.

This time he was content to sit in the boat, exhausted and relieved. They’d done it: Millhone and his daughter reclaimed the record he’d lost. It took them 17 days, 19 hours, 46 minutes, and 49 seconds, beating the 2003 record by more than nine hours.

The only question was how long it would stand.

* * *

Things looked good for Miller and his team. As they passed through towns, hundreds of people who had been following their progress online gathered along the banks to cheer them on. They were exhausted but determined. Now that Millhone was finished, they knew exactly what marks they had to hit.

And they were hitting them. By the time they got to Memphis, their lead over team Mile Marker Zero's time had grown to more than seven hours, with just a few days to go.

But over the next few days, weather started churning in the Gulf. North of the historic river town of Natchez, Mississippi, they battled thirty-mile-per-hour headwinds.

One morning, in a sustained wind of twenty-three miles per hour, waves crested over the canoe, filling it faster than they could bail. Whitaker, who was sleeping under the spray skirt, woke up and announced he was going to need a snorkel. They swerved in front of a barge to reach shore.

Fifty feet from land, they had taken on so much water that they couldn't steer. If they'd been another hundred feet from shore, Miller said, they wouldn't have made it.

The river wound back and forth. When the canoe turned out of the wind, they made up time. When it turned into it, they lost it. Their lead slipped from four hours to three, to two, and then to just thirty minutes.

When they fell fifteen minutes behind, they knew they had to do something drastic. Team Mississippi Speed Record was still forty-eight hours from the end, but the men decided to put all their paddles into the water. Once they did, none of them would sleep until they reached Mile Marker Zero.

The wind never stopped. Coming into New Orleans just after midnight, they knew they were in trouble: they were riding waves at least four feet high. The authorities had issued a warning for small craft to get off the river.

Again waves crashed over the gunnels. The team was stuck in the middle of the channel. They needed to get to either bank but couldn't, because there were ocean liners to one side and barges on the other. With every wave, the boat was filling, little by little. They were barely holding on.

Finally, they called the support boat over. They managed to pull up beside it without getting smashed. The paddlers held on to the side while trying to bail. Their arms were wrenched in the waves, and still they couldn't get the water out fast enough. There was nothing left to do. The cause was lost; the river had won.

Throwing what little they could onto the support boat, all four jumped aboard.

Miller watched as his canoe sank under the waves, curled around the back of the boat, and disappeared into the night.

* * *

By that time, Millhone had already been back in Minnesota for a few days. Sitting at home, he'd been thinking about his team's new world record and trying to figure out what it meant to him. When he got word of Miller's sinking, his mind immediately went to all the things that can go wrong on the river and to all the close calls his team experienced.

He sent Miller a text. It was the first time the two had been in touch in a long time. Millhone wrote that he was glad they were safe and sorry their attempt had ended that way. He said it made their disagreement seem petty.

Miller wrote back. He agreed that coming so close to dying put their dispute in perspective. He thanked Millhone for setting the bar so high and for helming a team of such worthy competitors.

Millhone replied, saying lunch was on him. He thanked Miller for sending him that first Facebook note years earlier, and for helping to get the whole adventure started.

"Never would have happened without you," Miller wrote. "Look forward to sharing stories some time."

"You guys had it," Millhone responded. "You deserve the record, but no one can take away the memories."

For Millhone, who has built a life on memories like those, the exchange was a gracious end to a long story.

But for Miller, the ending was bittersweet. He'd come so close. He had spent years getting to this point. And now he knew the river could be run faster—and that he could do it. So even as he began to pick up the pieces from this attempt, his mind turned, as inexorably as the river, to the next one.

CREWING THE RECORD

IN 2018, I SAW A SMALL NEWS ITEM ABOUT THREE MEN WHO were trying to break an old—and very fast—record for paddling down the Mississippi River. One of them was KJ Millhone, who had set an even earlier record of thirty-five days in 1980.

Now that record was down to eighteen days.

The Mississippi River has flowed through much my life. I grew up on the river in the town of Winona, Minnesota. We fished its backwaters. We jumped off its bridges. We water-skied up and down its main channel. The year before I contacted Millhone, our family had paddled down 125 miles of it. It seemed like this world record story would connect with many parts of my life. And if a record was going to be set, I wanted a front-row seat.

Millhone's 2018 attempt made it as far as Iowa. I got in touch with him and asked if he was planning to try again. He said he wasn't sure, but we stayed in touch. Later that year, he contacted me. He'd been thinking about another run for some time. When his eighteen-year-old daughter Casey asked to be part of any attempt, he decided to do it.

So I got an assignment for *Outside* to cover the story and met the team. It included an oncology nurse from Minneapolis named Scott Miller who in 2005 had paddled two thousand miles north, from Minneapolis to Hudson Bay, with another canoeist. I did all I could to get ready for their 2020 attempt. I went to watch the team train on the river. I did many interviews.

Then the pandemic hit. The team was bitterly divided on whether or not they should go. Millhone and Miller had a huge fight and went their separate ways.

After the 2020 attempt was scuttled, both teams set their sights on 2021. Yet by the spring Millhone was still short of support crew. He was set to launch in April, but at the last minute two "experienced river people" dropped out, and he got even shorter.

* * *

I was still planning to write about Millhone's and Miller's dueling attempts when I got the call. Under the guise of "getting the full story," Millhone offered me a spot on his support boat's day crew. He said I could meet the team in Minneapolis, then go down the rest of the river as part of the crew. He told me there would be no restrictions on my reporting.

I made sure he knew I would be writing about both teams, and that I had to give Miller a fair shake. He said that was fine. I told Miller the same, and he understood.

But I still wasn't sure. It had been only a month since my own near-death experience in the Mississippi River, when I tipped my canoe in forty-two-degree water. I was not eager to repeat that. I had a bad feeling about the whole thing. Plus it sounded miserable. There were only two people lined up for the day shift (including me, and I hadn't yet agreed) and two for the night shift. That would mean twelve hours on and twelve off for at least fourteen days. It left no room for error, illness, or accident. I also knew, having grown up on the river, just how dangerous it can be.

And yet, against the feeling in my gut, I accepted. After all, I'd been following this story for years.

Now I was part of it.

* * *

In the old days—let's say 1980—you could break the Mississippi paddling record if you had a friend or two willing to drive a car and make you peanut butter and jelly sandwiches along the way. You could stop and camp. You could miss your connections. It was hard. It was dangerous. But it wasn't overly complicated.

Yet as time went on, the record got faster, and there was less room for error. Tim Muhich was the leader of two teams that attempted to break it in both 2014 and 2017. I asked Muhich how difficult it was.

"You're paddling sixty strokes a minute, twelve hours on, four hours off," he told me. "During that time off you have to eat, do navigation, and sleep. You end up sleeping, at most, three and half hours in the bottom of a wet canoe. Then you get up and paddle sixty strokes a minute again for the next twelve hours. We were eating close to ten thousand calories a day, and we all still lost over a pound a day."

In 2003, Bob Bradford and Clark Eid reached Mile Marker Zero in 18 days, 4 hours, and 51 minutes. The two were a team competing in Eid's Mississippi River Challenge for Rett Syndrome and Leukodystrophy. They used a covered, two-person canoe; one slept while the other paddled. When I was researching the story, I called Eid, who told me there are two things you need to break the record: discipline and grit.

"You're putting yourself on a schedule," Eid says. "And you're pushing yourself past your limits. Your body goes into a state where you're eating every two hours. You're sleeping about four hours, and you'll hallucinate if you're pushing yourself right. You're going into a very unnatural state."

But today there is another thing you need: a support crew.

You need people to cook the food, manage the hydration, drive a support boat (or two), manage logistics, talk to barges and lockmasters, deal with human waste, manage social media, drive cars, reserve campsites, repair canoes, buy emergency supplies, handle medical issues, and on and on and on . . .

There are four paddlers in the boat, but there is a small army behind them. The modern support crew needs to be a military machine, a superorganism, a colossal group effort. And every crew member is a crucial link in the sometimes fragile chain pulling the canoe down the river.

* * *

On Thursday, April 22, 2021, Millhone's team launched the boat at Lake Itasca.

They had a rough start. Within the first twenty-four hours, Millhone got deathly ill and was vomiting. He had to take several hours off the water on the shore of Lake Winnibigoshish, while the team's doctor, Sami, hooked him up to an IV to rehydrate. There was some talk of going on without him. But Millhone rallied and got back in the boat, and they carried on.

The following Sunday, roughly four hundred miles downstream, I drove out to Millhone's home in Minnetonka, where his boat crew chief, a disheveled insomniac named Donavan, was frantically finishing work on the support boat. Also present were the night crew—two thirty-nine-year-olds, Derek and Tim, who had met in college.

The boat was an aging pontoon that would nearly kill us several times. It had been modified so that on one side hung a network of steel pipes that Donavan called the "cradle," which was raised and lowered with a winch. When the boat was in the water, the canoe slid into the cradle on rollers. Once it did, the paddlers could climb onto the pontoon, do their business (such as it was), then slide back out into the river.

In theory, this was not a bad idea.

In practice, however, we were asking more of it than it had to give. The pontoon was badly overloaded. It had two small freezers, a microwave, metal boxes for the paddlers' gear, a generator, and more. On the back were two tiny anchors, and underneath, in the middle of the boat, Donavan had mounted a third pontoon. This extra pontoon was slightly larger than the outer ones, so the boat rocked like a seesaw when you walked across it from left to right.

We tested the cradle once on Lake Minnetonka. None of the aforementioned gear was on the boat. We let the cradle down. The canoe slid in, then back out. It seemed to work.

And that was the extent of our training.

* * *

The next day, on Monday afternoon, we gathered at Hidden Falls Regional Park in St. Paul to meet the paddlers. While we waited for the canoe, Donavan shouted for things to be done in no particular order, and we attempted to do them.

It was late afternoon when the paddlers came around the bend and landed on the sandy shore. Lisa Millhone, our support crew leader and KJ's wife, worked to get them what they asked for. Then they took off down the river.

Once the canoe was out of sight, Donavan backed the pontoon down the boat ramp into the water. As it drifted off the trailer, everyone onshore noticed that the deck was just a few inches above the waterline.

Donavan, being the only one who knew how to run the boat, got on it with Derek and Tim for the night. It was just after 5:00 PM when they set off. As they motored downstream, the pontoon sat so low in the water that it seemed like it was about to sink. It was supposed to travel well over twice as fast as the paddlers, but it could barely catch up with the canoe.

A few miles downstream, the crew offloaded some of the freezers and other unnecessary equipment. But that night, after darkness fell, while attempting to stop on Lake Pepin, they dropped both anchors off the back of the boat. Immediately, the current starting pulling the craft underwater. Millhone watched in horror as the engine and both gas tanks dipped under the water and the bow tilted upward. Then, at the last minute, the anchors popped loose and the pontoon bobbed back to the surface.

* * *

The next morning, I arrived in Lake City for my day shift on the support boat.

Sitting onshore at the Lake City marina, which juts out into Lake Pepin, I heard sirens. For a minute, I thought there was a tornado, but the sky was clear and the air was still. Then a rescue boat raced out from the marina across the water, toward what looked like the pontoon. A few minutes later, it came back empty-handed.

When the support boat limped into port, Derek and Tim were

laughing because someone had called in the Mayday. They thought the pontoon was sinking. We pulled the boat out on the trailer. In the parking lot, Donavan unscrewed the plugs on the pontoons. For several minutes, water drained out of them onto the ground.

As it turned out, it was sinking.

* * *

The canoe sped on. After Millhone's initial collapse, he returned to something like health, and they picked up speed. By the time they hit Minneapolis, they were ten hours ahead of the 2003 record.

Meanwhile, with the pontoon off the water, we on the support crew scrambled to organize a new support plan. Since I grew up on the river, I was tasked with finding landings to meet the paddlers.

South of Lake City, we moved through the so-called Driftless Area, with green hills rising up on each side of the river. Lisa located an aluminum welder in Winona who said he could fix the pontoons. But we still couldn't get it back on the water until Guttenberg, Iowa, late the next day.

There, around 6:00 PM, the canoe pushed off. Once again, Donavan backed the pontoon into the water. It still tilted badly to the right.

Being on the day shift, I assumed I would meet the support boat in the morning. But Donavan turned to me. "Frank," he said, "you're going on the boat with these guys for a few hours. I want you to run through a few cycles before we take it out tomorrow."

"Where will I get off?"

"Don't worry about that!" he said. "We'll figure it out."

I did worry about it. Sami, the team doctor, gave me a look of pity.

The sun was setting when I climbed on the pontoon with Derek and Tim. The river was calm. Ahead of us, the paddlers moved downstream. We had radio headsets to communicate with them, and Millhone was telling stories from his 1980 trip. The hills along the river got lower. The sound of a train horn came from across the valley. An eagle flew so close we could hear its wings.

It was beautiful. It was almost peaceful, but there was something else I felt. It wasn't quite dread. But I knew I didn't want to be on the river at night, and that I hadn't really been given a choice.

The river was flooded, so there was lots of debris. The water temperature was in the fifties. I knew if anything happened to the boat, we'd be in trouble. It was too late, but I wondered if I hadn't made a huge mistake.

Clouds moved in. The sun set. Soon the team told us they needed a shift change, so we went ahead to look for a spot. Derek steered toward the side of the river. I was told to throw the anchor off the back.

When it caught, the rope burned through my bare hands and we slipped downstream. It was like trying to hold a Mack Truck.

Tim grabbed the rope behind me and wrapped it around his arm. "Don't wrap it around your arm!" I yelled.

He unwrapped it, and we pulled. The boat stopped. Derek throttled in reverse, and the back end plowed underwater. "Stop!" I yelled. "We're sinking!"

He eased up, adjusted the motor, then started more slowly while Tim and I pulled. The engine was half-submerged, but eventually we made it back up to the anchor and it came loose.

Derek steered us behind an island where there was no current. Tim threw the anchor, but this time we didn't even move. We lowered the cradle.

When the canoe arrived, it rolled in. The four paddlers climbed onboard and the deck sank to just above the water. They changed clothes. They ate. They used the "luggable loos." Then they got back in the canoe and set off.

After we'd cleaned up, we started the engine and passed the canoe, looking for a landing where I could get off. The river ahead was pitch black. I turned to Derek. "Shouldn't we use the floodlights to look for logs?" I asked.

"No," he said, "We're only supposed to use those for docking."

I shrugged. It wasn't a discussion, and he had the wheel.

A few minutes later, I was sitting next to the front railing when a massive green shape materialized in front of the boat, a few feet from my head.

BOOM!!!

BOOM!!!

BOOM!!!

"Oh shit!" Derek yelled. "What was that?"

"A buoy," I said.

The boat stopped. At first, it seemed like we'd lost our motor. But when Derek pushed the throttle, the boat moved a little. "I think we lost the depth finder," he said, looking at the display.

Cautiously, he brought us back up to speed. I was told to stand up front and look for buoys, still with no floodlights. So for several hours, I scanned the inky black looking for buoys and logs and hoped the water was deep enough.

We found two landings, but both were blocked by railroad bridges, which our canopy couldn't pass under. Around midnight, we finally came to a ramp where I was able get a ride into town with Donavan.

The next morning, the pontoon puttered into Savanna, Illinois. When we pulled it out on the trailer, the right pontoon was full of water again.

Sami turned to me. "I think we've seen the last of this boat," he said. "But maybe we should put a few more holes in it to be sure."

* * *

With the boat out of commission for good, we were back to ground support. That meant trying to stay one step ahead of the canoe, with meals and water and clothes and whatever else the paddlers might need.

This was our Plan B. But there really was no Plan B. We had no maps, no list of boat ramps, and no contingency plans. Instead we scanned Google Earth to try to figure out if something was a road, an access point, or a launch. Sometimes this worked. Other times there was fencing you couldn't see in the satellite photos. Or else the photos had been taken in low water, and the landing was deep under high water.

But the canoe never stopped, so neither did we. The cooks cooked. Sami and I white-knuckled it to the next boat launch. We got lost on back roads. We probably drove three times as many miles as the canoe paddled, trying to find obscure launches in swamps and backwoods.

Morale declined. We were all stressed. No one slept much. It was unclear who was in charge. Divisions started to arise, as some crew members felt others were being treated better.

To make matters worse, without the support boat, our lead over the 2003 record time started to slip. By the time we got to Cairo, Illinois, our chances for breaking the record were in serious doubt.

Cairo is where the Ohio River pours into the Mississippi. The flow of water there can be tremendous. In 2003 Bob Bradford and Clark Eid got a massive push from a flooded Ohio.

Cairo is also one of the most depressing cities in America, an exemplar of Rust Belt blight. The place was full of burned-out building, empty houses, and abandoned storefronts. Once fifteen thousand people lived there. Now fewer than two thousand did. It looked like a bomb had gone off in the middle of town.

Somewhere in Iowa, Lisa had purchased a brand-new pontoon. But it took Donavan several days to transfer all the equipment and to reinstall the cradle. We launched it in Hannibal, Missouri, but the electrical system wasn't working. So out it came for another few days until the wiring was fixed.

The new boat finally went in the water at a state park in southern Missouri. Donavan and Lisa took the first shift, piloting it down to Cairo. There, at the point of land between the Mississippi and Ohio Rivers, is a park.

Tim and Derek and I drove there to look for a place the pontoon could land, so they could get on for the night shift. But the shore was the worst combination of mud and rocks. So we drove across the Ohio to Wickliffe, Kentucky, where we found a boat ramp that would work. We lay in the parking lot sleeping, until the new pontoon arrived around 1:00 AM.

Derek and Tim got on.

Donavan and Lisa got off.

Then three of us went south to Hayti, Missouri, where we checked into a nasty hotel with sticky carpets.

Late that night, a massive storm rolled through. The paddlers and the new support boat were trapped on an island for several hours until it blew over.

* * *

We moved south. The new support boat didn't sink. It didn't lean ominously to one side. It could go faster than eleven miles per hour. Yet it still didn't seem to be saving much time.

One day, as we wound along between Arkansas and Mississippi, I finally got to actually be on the day crew. I'd never seen the river south of Iowa, and I had always pictured the Lower Mississippi as an industrial wasteland. But it was quite the opposite: a vast wilderness, with wide islands and pristine sand beaches.

Other than on barges, there wasn't a person for miles around. If Huck and Jim had come drifting around a bend, it would have seemed like the most natural thing in the world. When I asked Millhone how the river looked compared to in 1980, he said it looked better. For a few hours, I was almost able to relax and enjoy the ride. Maybe I was glad I came after all.

Yet there was still a sense of urgency. We were losing time. The canoe was stopping for too long. Frustration was growing.

Then around Greenville, Mississippi, the weather improved. The wind calmed. The transitions got faster. And by the time we hit Baton Rouge—where ship traffic had ramped up—our lead over the 2003 time was back up to nine hours.

The next day we came into New Orleans. Donavan and I were getting on the pontoon at the dock of a small transport company. "Is it true," I asked one of the pilots, "that you guys call canoers 'suicide jockeys'?"

"Yeah!" he said. He laughed. "That's true."

"What else do you call them?"

"Dumbasses," he said. "I mean, the river is relentless. We watch boats capsize out here. If you go in, even with a life jacket, it's no more than a fifty-fifty chance."

Soon the pontoon arrived. We took the empty food bags off and threw the full ones on.

Then Donavan and I sped off to catch up with the dumbasses.

* * *

The end was in sight. We had less than a hundred miles to go. But just south of New Orleans, the team wanted to change positions. We looked for a place to anchor out of the ship traffic. There were a few barges parked along the right bank. Donavan aimed for an opening between them. As we neared shore, there was a BANG under the boat, followed by a long, ugly scraping sound.

The boat stopped.

"Rock!" Donavan yelled. "We're hung up!"

He gunned the motor. There was another grinding sound. He went back and raised the motor. Chunks of the propeller were missing. "Motor's gone!" he said. He threw up his hands. "We're screwed! We're done!"

The canoe arrived. Stuck there on the rocks, we lowered the cradle. The paddlers climbed out, got some supplies, then climbed back in and paddled on.

It was almost noon. They had seventy miles left, but the river was a freeway of oceangoing vessels. When night came, they would have no lights or food. I watched as they sped on, getting smaller and smaller. They were on their way to the end of the river, alone.

Suddenly, the pontoon started drifting. Somehow we had come loose. Donavan tried the motor. The propeller spun, but the boat didn't move. There were ships and barges everywhere around us, and we had no way to avoid drifting into their path.

Donavan got on the radio and issued a Mayday.

A dispatcher responded. "We've got a pleasure craft that's lost power," he said. "Is there anyone in the area who can assist?"

Within minutes, an enormous tug arrived and was pulling us back upstream.

* * *

Sami met us at the dock. He and I took everything the paddlers might need, threw them in his RV, and raced south. We scoured

Google Earth for some place where we could give the paddlers their lights, extra seat, food, and water for their last miles.

The Mississippi Delta, however, has almost no public boat landings. We found one, and I stepped over a dead alligator to check it out, but it was blocked with boulders. We found another, but it was completely hidden from upstream. The paddlers never would have seen it in time.

The sun was low. Casey texted us a location. I looked at the map: it seemed to be where a road went down to the water.

When Sami and I got there, it turned out to be a ferry terminal . . . and our last shot. If we didn't catch them here, they would be heading into the night through the ships, with a very bad storm predicted to roll in.

A ferry was docked at the terminal. Cars were driving onto it. When the final vehicle had boarded, I asked one of the workers if we could use the dock to hand off some supplies to our canoe.

"I suppose," he said, "but this is the last ferry for the day. After this, we lock the gate, and we're done."

Then, without ceremony, he swung the gates closed, locked them, and got on the ferry. It left.

The canoe was ten minutes upstream. There was barbed wire along the top of the fence, but one section hung over the water. I shook it. A small space opened. I climbed out over the water and pushed my head through it. Then my torso. Then my legs. On the other side, I climbed back to the dock.

Through a narrow space under the gate, Sami shoved all the gear and food. Then I ran it down to the water.

Within minutes the canoe arrived. I gave them the food and rain gear, lights and batteries. Bobby handed back some things he didn't want yet.

"We'll take the rest of this in Venice," he said.

I had no idea where Venice was. To my knowledge, we hadn't planned that far ahead.

"You are meeting us in Venice, aren't you?" he asked.

"I . . . don't know."

Bobby lost it. "What do you mean you don't know?!? Somebody's meeting us in Venice, right?"

Casey called Lisa. I couldn't hear what she said, but the paddlers quickly got back in the boat and left. By then, it was nearly dark.

Just then a truck pulled up. Out jumped Derek with a guy named Joey Cargol, who was trailering a small boat. They grabbed everything the paddlers might need, got back in their car, and sped south. I guessed they were going to Venice.

Sami and I picked up all that was left and threw it in his RV. Then we drove south. Venice, it turned out, was the last town on the road south. From the Venice marina, Lisa had booked another small boat to head out to Mile Marker Zero. But with a massive storm rolling in, there was no telling what would happen if we got caught in the wide-open delta.

In the parking lot, the support crew gathered to talk to the captain.

"I initially didn't want to make this trip," he told us. "And I tried to find a bigger boat. But this was all I could find. There is a risk of severe weather. I have to tell you all that. So if you'd rather not go, I understand."

Sami decided to go.

I considered it. After all, we had come this far. It seemed like a shame not to go all the way. And yet, I was exhausted, physically and emotionally. I'd never had so many close calls in all my life, and I didn't know if I could handle another one. I pictured the small boat being tossed on giant waves, with lightning, thunder, high winds, and no land in sight.

I waved to Sami as he and the others motored out of the harbor, into the river, into the night. Then I crawled into the RV and crashed.

* * *

The storm passed just north of Mile Marker Zero, leaving several inches of standing water on the roads outside Venice. The canoe beat the 2003 record by more than nine hours.

To me, the fact that they did felt like a miracle. So many times, the whole effort hung by the thinnest thread. Every person on the support crew saved the attempt at least once. To this day, I don't quite know how we pulled it off, with so many things having gone so wrong.

* * *

Around 5:00 AM in Venice, the boats all came back into the marina from Mile Marker Zero.

There was no announcement.

There was no celebration.

There was no sense of jubilation.

There was relief.

There was exhaustion.

After everyone was off the boats, the paddlers crawled into the vehicles and fell asleep.

I, on the other hand, was well rested. So I took the wheel of Sami's RV, hit the gas, and started the long drive home.

A RACE FOR REDEMPTION

IN 2021, TWO WEEKS AFTER SCOTT MILLER LOST HIS CANOE, his world record attempt, and nearly his life, he sat down with his crew chief, Michael "Moose" Dougherty, at an Irish bar. Over pints of Guinness, Miller made his pitch. "I'm not going to beat around the bush," he said. "I'm going again, and I need you to be crew chief."

Dougherty suspected this was coming. Before driving to the bar, he had planned to say no. He even told his wife there was no way he could do another attempt. A Mississippi River paddle is a huge project, with many risks.

And yet, Dougherty heard the words come out of his mouth like someone else was saying them. "OK," he told Miller. "I'll do it."

They decided to plan for the spring of 2023. That would be the year they would try to take the record from KJ Millhone, which stood at 17 days, 19 hours, and 46 minutes.

In the aftermath of Miller's 2021 failure, his mind ran over all that had gone right (teamwork, planning, organization), all that had gone wrong (weather), and all that could be improved (some canoe modifications, simplifying food and hydration, streamlining gear).

Miller knew he could do better. So he started over with a new boat, new paddlers, and a new plan and with Dougherty—a marathoner, a Leadville Trail 100 Run mountain biker, and a retired corporate public affairs flack who knew how to get things done.

Next, Miller started looking for team members, which he found in high-level racers: Paul Cox, a digital media editor who was the two-time winner—and record holder—of the Great Alabama 650 Paddle Race. Wally Werderich, a Chicago public defender who had placed second and third in the Missouri River 340 and had two national "Stock C1" titles. And Judd Steinback, the 2022 masters national champion for men's and mixed canoes, who had raced everything from the 175-mile Ruta Maya Belize River Challenge to the 120-mile AuSable River Canoe Marathon.

Waiting in the wings as backup paddler was Joe Mann, winner of both the MR 340 and the Alabama 650.

These were some of the best paddlers around. With good weather, good water, and good luck—well, if they couldn't break Millhone's 2021 record, no one could.

The team planned to launch on May 3, 2023. But the long winter with heavy snow cover meant Lake Winnibigoshish, a huge shallow lake on their route, was still choked with ice. They would need to cross its sixteen miles in their first twenty-four hours. Even without ice, Winnibigoshish is one of the most dangerous places on the river. A slight wind can result in huge waves.

They pushed the launch back to May 7. In early May the team and support crew gathered at Dougherty's cabin in northern Minnesota, which would serve as base camp for the first leg of the attempt, since nearly seven hundred miles of the Mississippi are in the state.

Then they waited. Every day, someone went to check the ice. Every day it was still there. With each new report, the initial excitement waned and a restlessness grew. The paddlers and crew sat around. Every conversation became about ice, rife with wild speculation about the sun, about where the wind might blow the ice, and about when ice-out would happen. Everyone had deadlines, jobs and lives to return to. Werderich, as a lawyer, had a small window in which to launch. If they couldn't go by May 11, he was out.

Finally, on May 9, the paddlers took the canoe to Winnibigoshish. They found the lake was mostly clear, except for about a mile left of "candle ice," which crumbles and can be plowed through if necessary. The choice was clear: go now, or don't go at all.

The launch was on.

That afternoon, members of Miller's twenty-plus-person support crew drove to Lake Itasca, the headwaters of the Mississippi River. There they set up camp, while the four paddlers attempted to get one last night of sleep.

The next morning at 3:30 AM, the support crew woke up in their tents, jumped out, and started getting the canoe ready to put in the water.

The boat was a twenty-three-foot Wenonah Minnesota 4—the same model used on Miller's previous attempt—only with several modifications. Like the previous boat, the new one had bulkheads installed to help keep water out of the middle two seats. For much of the journey, three of the men would paddle while the fourth slept in the boat. It also had a new battery system to power the lights, an iPad for navigation, and GPS trackers.

Daylight filtered through the trees. The support crew wheeled the canoe down to the water. The four men got in and paddled across Lake Itasca to the row of large stones where the lake spills over and the Mississippi River officially begins. Once there, they got out and took some photos. Then at 6:00 AM, the paddlers walked the canoe over the rocks and past a small footbridge, got in, and—they were off.

The water was high and fast. The canoe wound through the marshes, following the river. Almost immediately, they started picking up time. After the first morning, they were ahead of the 2021 record pace by an hour. By evening they arrived in the city of Bemidji, where the support crew put on the spray skirts and switched out the battery powering the electronics and lights.

Around 5:00 PM, they started across Lake Bemidji. The ice had just gone out there too, and the water temperature was forty-six degrees—deadly cold if the canoe flipped and they couldn't get back in.

By 1:30 AM, they arrived at Lake Winnibigoshish. The ice was gone. They were able to cut straight across the sixteen miles. At first, the water was smooth and glassy. But as they rounded the last corner, with several miles to go, the wind kicked up. The waves got bigger and bigger and pounded the canoe. Still, when they reached the other side, they were four hours and twenty minutes ahead of the record pace.

The river turned south. The water was still dangerously high. The dams were raging. In some places, the paddlers could cut straight through the flooded forest. Their lead grew to five hours.

Then six.

Then seven.

By the time they reached Minneapolis in the middle of the night, they were twelve hours ahead of the record pace. But the river gives, and the river takes. Though twelve hours was a good lead, Miller knew it could disappear in a day with bad weather, canoe repair, medical emergencies, or worse.

In St. Paul, the team picked up two support boats, which would follow them all the way to the end, if they made it that far. The next day, they reached Lake Pepin, another shallow, dangerous lake. For five hours the canoe was pounded by headwinds gusting up to sixteen miles per hour. The team battled four-foot waves as they struggled across the lake's twenty-two miles.

In 2021, both Millhone's and Miller's teams were hit with huge storms and high winds that ended Miller's attempt and nearly ended Millhone's. But in 2023, the river was kinder. The paddlers had one night of cold, soaking rain, but as they moved south the sky cleared and the water was calm. That fact, combined with the high water, the caliber of the paddlers, and the efficiency of Moose's machine, meant they kept piling on time. Every waypoint felt like a victory, with another hour gained on the record. By the time they reached Iowa they were twenty hours ahead.

The job, however, was the same: one stroke after another—more than a million, by some counts—down all 2,350 miles of the Mississippi. Eat, drink, sleep, excrete (don't ask), and paddle.

With four guys living together in such close quarters, the canoe was like a soggy bachelor pad. There was a slurry in the bottom that they called "people soup." No motorized bailer was powerful enough to expel it. Instead, the heroic support crew would occasionally empty the boat and try to reestablish a modicum of hygiene.

On most days, the heavy current was a blessing. But late one night at Lock and Dam 15 in Iowa, it was not. The paddlers were waiting to pass through the lock. A barge was struggling to come upstream out of the lock, so the lockmaster told them to move to river right, directly above the dam. Miller and Steinback were paddling while Werderich and Cox slept. They paddled over to where the lockmaster directed them. But once they reached the sheer concrete wall on that side, the current was so strong it started pulling them toward the dam. The river was too powerful.

"It was like a thousand-percent sprint, and we were slowly drifting backwards," says Steinback. "It was one of the most harrowing moments of my entire life."

Werderich and Cox woke up to Steinback's yell: "Get up, now!" They grabbed their paddles. But even with the added muscle, the team couldn't hold their place. So they radioed the support boat, which came over. They held on to the boat while it struggled upstream against the current, until the barge was clear and they could finally paddle back down into the lock.

It was a close call, but Mississippi River record attempts are full of close calls. In a flash, the big, slow, muddy water can become the most dangerous place in the world. "I woke up like every night to—I don't want to say screams from above," says Cox, "but let's say, urgent commands."

Badly shaken, the paddlers decided to rest below the dam. They spent about three hours sleeping and collecting their nerves before they paddled on.

They quickly gained back those three hours, plus another ten.

For several days their lead over the 2021 record hovered around thirty hours. But as they got closer to the Gulf of Mexico, the team started getting hammered with barge traffic and oceangoing ships. On several occasions, they stopped to let the massive boats pass. "When you get down to Baton Rouge," says Cox, "it's like you're playing Frogger trying to get across. You're a tiny little blip on the radar screen."

With a thirty-one-hour lead, the paddlers decided to use the time wisely to avoid the barges and ships. As a result, their lead dropped to twenty-eight, to twenty-five as they got closer to Louisiana. North of Baton Rouge, it fell to 22:47, even though they were paddling up to 170 miles a day.

Then, with just over two hundred miles left, they started to claw back time, and they pushed their lead back up over twenty-three hours. They passed the place where Miller sank in 2021. They sped through New Orleans, then through the huge bends in the river further south.

On Friday, May 26, as night fell, they reached the last stretch. Around 2:00 AM on Saturday, they came into the area known as the Head of Passes, where the river splits into three channels. There sits the rickety wooden structure called Mile Marker Zero, which marks the official end of the Mississippi River.

Alongside the canoe were several boats, including one loaded with cheering family and support crew. Yet even then, Miller knew it wasn't over. "I couldn't let myself feel like we had it in the bag until the very end," he says. "There are so many things that can happen at any moment. Even in the last two hours when the guys went into this freight train trance, I was like, *Oh my God, we're going to hit a buoy!* We didn't know exactly where we were going, and everybody was screaming and yelling which light to aim for."

"It was surreal," says Werderich. "There were all of these noises from the boats around us. There were spotlights on us."

Finally someone found the right light, and they headed for it. At 2:15 AM, they arrived at Mile Marker Zero. They tied up the boat; then all four paddlers—Cox, Werderich, Steinback, and Miller—climbed on the platform.

"When we got to the actual mile marker," says Steinback, "I was crying because there were so many emotions. It was all adrenaline, euphoria, gratitude, and just immense fatigue. But when I climbed up on Mile Marker Zero, I felt weightless. Like there was no effort at all."

The air was filled with the cheers and air horns—celebration and victory. They had beaten the 2021 record by twenty-three hours and thirty minutes, setting a new standard of 16 days, 20 hours, and 16 minutes.

On top of Mile Marker Zero, in a small waterproof box, there's a logbook that anyone who reaches the end of the river can sign. The paddlers opened it and signed their names. "When we signed that log," says Steinback, "it really felt like we'd just made history."

For Miller, it felt like that and more. "To have all those people cheering," he says, "it felt like we just won the Super Bowl or something. It was just so much more amazing of an ending than I ever could have imagined."

ACKNOWLEDGMENTS

I owe debts to many people for the creation of this book. First and foremost, I want to thank Hunter Smoak and Jake Abrahams for being on the river that morning. I want to thank them for having a throw rope, for being prepared, and for their calm manner and steady paddling. Without them, I wouldn't be here to write any of this.

Thanks also to my editor at the Minneapolis *Star Tribune*, Bob Timmons, for letting me tell that story. My hope is that it saved a life or two, and that there were news stories of cold water drownings that we never read because it. But if nothing else, the publication also helped me find those mystery saviors in the red Mad River canoe.

Thanks to my wife, Bridgit, and daughters, Libby and Josie, for coming when I called, for warming me up, and for giving my life so much more meaning than it would otherwise have. I can't believe I came so close to leaving you behind. And thanks also to you three for always being game to go on a long hike with no training, and to get in a canoe and head down the river, never quite knowing where it will take us.

Thank you to Ann Regan, the legendary editor at the Minnesota Historical Society Press, who took me on, probably against her better judgment, as one of her last projects on her way out the door to retirement. It was a leap of faith on her part, and one that I'm glad she took. I hope we've created something of value for future generations of paddlers, of readers, of Minnesotans—and for anyone who loves being out on the water.

Thank you to the staff at the Minnesota Historical Society's Gale Library for enduring my questions, for retrieving endless canoe derby–related documents and artifacts, and for compiling an amazing newspaper database, without which the story of the Paul Bunyan Aquatennial Canoe Derby might have been lost. Thank you also to Lilah Crow of the Itasca County Historical Society for going above and beyond, digging up, scanning, and sending whatever she could find about Jesse Tibbetts and, his brothers, sons, and family.

Thanks to KJ Millhone for letting me have a front row seat to your crazy dream. Thanks to Sami Diab for all the laughter and for keeping me sane. Thanks to Lisa Millhone for running the crew with very long odds, against which few would have succeeded. Thanks to the cooks, Paul and Kris Dobbel, and Tom and Geri Herges, for the great food, laughter, and vodka gimlets in the camper, which I will always remember fondly.

Thanks to Scott Miller for letting me tag along on your adventures, and for all you've done to create a community on the water. Thanks also to Moose Dougherty, to Brad Sjostrom, and to Traci Danner-Bernadt, and to all the crew for an unforgettable time racing down the Mississippi in 2023. And thank you to the four paddlers—Scott Miller, Judd Steinback, Paul Cox, and Wally Werderich—for being so decent and fun to be around.

Thanks to the nameless builders who invented the canoe, and to the native craftspeople who created and mastered the canoe, and canoe building, over thousands of years.

Thanks to Bill Smith for taking so much time to remember the derby and answer endless questions about it, and for telling the story of Jim and Bernie Smith, which would otherwise have slipped away. Thanks to Stan Droogsma and Harlow Thompson for taking precious minutes to relive their derby memories. And thanks to all the Paul Bunyan Canoe Derby racers and their families. We owe you more than you could have dreamed.

Lastly, to the Mississippi River itself, and whatever spirits might live there, thank you for granting me, and those I love, permission and safe passage so far.

APPENDIX A

The History of the Mississippi Record

Clark Eid, the 2003 world co–record holder for paddling down the Mississippi, has made it his mission to document all Mississippi River paddling attempts and records through the years. Here is a condensed overview of Eid's history; later attempts are supplemented with my own reporting.

The 2021 dual attempt is covered in "An Epic Battle" and "Crewing the Record." The 2023 attempt is covered in "A Race for Redemption."

1881, FALSE FIRST RECORD

Willard Glazier (age 40 in 1881) claimed to be the first person to canoe the entire river and to have discovered its overlooked source. He published a book titled *Down the Great River: Embracing an Account of the Discovery of the True Source of the Mississippi* (Philadelphia, PA: Hubbard Brothers, 1891), but it was soon discovered that Glazier had plagiarized other expedition reports, and his claim was discredited by both the Minnesota state legislature and the Minnesota Historical Society.

1921, ATTEMPT (END: HANNIBAL, MISSOURI)

John Koors and Louis Neumann (ages unknown) started from Bemidji, Minnesota, on June 14 and ended sometime on or before

July 25, when they overturned after striking a wing dam near Hannibal.

1925, RECORD: 105 DAYS

Journalist Albert S. Tousley (26) paddled down the river with three different partners. He detailed his journey in *Where Goes the River* (Iowa City, IA: Tepee Press, 1928).

1937, ATTEMPT (END: GREENVILLE, MISSISSIPPI)

Glenn Gunderson (23) and Emerson Gonnsen (21), sophomores at Wheaton College, began their run on May 22, 1937. Their canoe capsized 1,900 miles later, on August 1, in a giant whirlpool near Greenville, Mississippi, and Gonnsen drowned near Mile Marker 576 on present-day river charts. Their seventeen-foot, seventy-five-pound canoe, named *Mississippi: Source to Sea*, was later recovered and sold for $20 near Greenville, to provide Gunderson with money for clothes and transportation home.

1937, 1ST GUINNESS RECORD: 49 DAYS ON THE WATER (56 DAYS TOTAL)

On July 4, after Gunderson and Gonnsen launched, the Memphis team of Joe Laughlin Tagg Jr. (17), Gerald M. Capers Jr. (28), and Charles David Saunders (17) set out from Itasca, reaching New Orleans on August 28 in 56 days. (*Guinness* says 49 days, but the team was off the water in St. Paul, Memphis, and Greenville for several days, so the total time elapsed was 56 days.) Tagg and Saunders were both high school seniors at the time. Their trip was detailed in the second half of Capers's book *The Mississippi River: Before and After Mark Twain* (Hicksville, NY: Exposition Press, 1977). This record was included in the *Guinness Book of World Records* in the 1970s.

1978, 2ND GUINNESS RECORD: 42 DAYS, 4 HOURS, 59 MINUTES

The British Royal Air Force team of Brian Smith (34), Peter Dodd (22), Mac Macboyle (23), Terry Riley (21), John (Steve) Stevenson (38), and Steve Pinkham (26) set the Guinness World Record using tandem kayaks, reaching Mile Marker Zero after 42 days, 4 hours, and 59 minutes. The record-setting event was part of the Royal Air

Force Diamond Jubilee. The paddlers needed to qualify for the team through racing trials in England.

1980, 3RD GUINNESS RECORD: 35 DAYS, 11 HOURS, 27 MINUTES
Steven M. Eckelkamp (23) and KJ Millhone (21) of Minnesota set the Guinness World Record. Their two-man support crew drove a car pulling a trailer for equipment. Their run was the last time that an open canoe, without a rudder, was used to set the record.

1984, 4TH GUINNESS RECORD, FIRSTS: 23 DAYS, 10 HOURS, 20 MINUTES
Verlen Kruger (61) and Valerie Fons (33) set the Guinness World Record during the Eddie Bauer Mississippi Challenge, which was cosponsored by Mad River Canoe. This was the first attempt that used a deliberate strategy to sleep one paddler in the canoe while the other paddler kept the canoe moving on the river.

1989, 5TH GUINNESS RECORD: 23 DAYS, 9 HOURS, 51 MINUTES
Bill Perdzock (25) and Mike Schnitzka (25) set the Guinness World Record. Schnitzka wrote about their record run in chapter four of his 2017 book, *Escaping the Velvet Rut: An Adventurer's Guide to Chasing Your Dreams*. When they reached Baton Rouge, they removed all extra weight from the canoe and made a tremendous sprint to Mile Marker Zero, reaching their goal only thirty minutes faster than the existing record time set by Kruger and Fons.

2001, ATTEMPT: 24 DAYS, 17 HOURS, 51 MINUTES
In 2001, the Great Mississippi River Race for Rett Syndrome was organized by Clark Eid and his wife, Mary Potter, in honor of their daughter Amanda to raise awareness and research funds for Rett syndrome. Using a fabric-decked Kruger Cruiser with rudder, canoeing legends Verlen Kruger (78) and Bob Bradford (58) won the race in 24 days, 17 hours, and 51 minutes. Record flooding and storms challenged all five starting teams. Miscommunication between the US Coast Guard and local law enforcement caused a significant delay when teams were forced off the river due to severe flooding.

2001, ATTEMPT: 26 DAYS, 6 HOURS, 40 MINUTES

Clark Eid (40) and Kurt Zimmermann (58) finished second in the Great Mississippi River Race for Rett Syndrome in 26 days, 6 hours, and 40 minutes. Their kayak (built by Eid) was christened the Double Helix, and at 25½ feet long, it is the longest canoe or kayak to successfully run the entire river. It was donated to the Tunica RiverPark & Museum in Tunica, Mississippi.

2003, 6TH GUINNESS RECORD: 18 DAYS, 4 HOURS, 51 MINUTES

The Mississippi River Challenge for Rett Syndrome and Leukodystrophy took place, with all funds raised supporting research for these two rare diseases. Clark Eid (42) and Bob Bradford (60), supported by a road crew led by Stan Hanson, set the Guinness World Record. The team used a full, fabric-decked Kruger Cruiser canoe outfitted with a rudder that could be controlled from either the bow or stern. Verlen Kruger was a race advisor. More at www.BeyondTheFinish.org.

2014, ATTEMPT (END: NATCHEZ, MISSISSIPPI)

In 2014, Tim Muhich (23), Clinton Adams (24), Colin Bright (mid-20s), and Boot Baweja (early 20s) made their first attempt. They got as far as Natchez, Mississippi, where they pulled off the water due to heavy rain, flash flooding, and nearby lightning strikes. While they waited out the weather, their time expired, and they ended their attempt, as they all had other obligations to return to.

2014, SOLO FEMALE RECORD: 102 DAYS

Grace Kluesner (24) is believed to be the first woman to solo canoe the Mississippi River. She completed the run in 102 days during the months of September, October, and November of 2014.

2015, MISSISSIPPI PADDLING AGE RECORD: 80 YEARS OLD

Dale Sanders (80) became the oldest person to canoe the entire Mississippi River. His run, which took eighty days, was made to raise awareness for juvenile diabetes.

2016, SOLO FEMALE RECORD: 65 DAYS

Janet Moreland (59) solo kayaked the Mississippi River from May 25 to July 28.

2017, ATTEMPT (END: GREENVILLE, MISSISSIPPI)

Tim Muhich (27) led another four-man team of Clinton Adams (27), Colin Bright (mid-20s), and Dale Waldo (mid-20s). They set the fastest recorded pace recorded to date on the upper river sections, outpacing the 2003 Guinness World Record by twenty-four hours by New Boston, Illinois. Poor weather near Burlington and Nauvoo, Illinois, eroded their time advantage; by Cairo, Illinois, they realized they could not make up the time. Around thirty miles upstream from Greenville, Mississippi, Adams came down with heatstroke, forcing them to stop.

2018, ATTEMPT (END: GUTTENBERG, IOWA)

KJ Millhone (59), Kevin Eckelkamp (23), and Nate Lastinger (27) were the first three-man team since 1937 to try setting the record. Lastinger was raising awareness of heart disease and funds for the American Heart Association. Unfortunately, he had to depart from the team after Lake Pepin, Minnesota, due to his son's illness. The remaining paddlers continued to Guttenberg, Iowa, before officially stopping. The run's pace lagged the 2003 record pace by five hours at the Lake Winnibigoshish Dam and progressed to an eleven-hour deficit by the outlet of Lake Pepin. Kevin was the nephew of the late Steven M. Eckelkamp, the 1980 record coholder with Millhone.

2020, BIRCHBARK CANOE RECORD

Dustin Stensland (31) became the first person on record to travel the entire Mississippi River in a birchbark canoe. He started on June 19 and ended October 4.

2020, MISSISSIPPI PADDLING AGE RECORD: 81 YEARS OLD

Stan Stark (81) became the oldest person to canoe the entire Mississippi River, breaking Dale Sanders's 2015 record. He started on July 14 and ended on November 3, making the trip in 111 days.

2021, 7TH GUINNESS RECORD: 17 DAYS, 19 HOURS, 46 MINUTES

KJ Millhone (62), Casey Millhone (20), Rod Price (60), and Bobby Johnson (43) of Team Mile Marker Zero set the Guinness World Record of 17 days, 19 hours, and 46 minutes. Their run had an on-water support craft. The record is covered at length in the chapters "An Epic Battle" and "Crewing the Record."

2021, ATTEMPT (ENDED JUST NORTH OF NEW ORLEANS)

Scott Miller (45), Joel Ford (36), Perry Whitaker (59), and Adam Macht (34) of Team Mississippi Speed Record started their run on May 4, soon after the Millhone team. High winds and waves north of New Orleans caused them to founder. Their canoe was lost and the attempt terminated, as detailed in the chapter "An Epic Battle."

2021, SOLO FEMALE RECORD: 55 DAYS, 8 HOURS, 17 MINUTES

Traci Lynn Martin (48) achieved this record from May 17 to July 11. Martin, known as the "Mississippi Mermaid," has rheumatoid arthritis.

2022, 1ST GUINNESS MISSISSIPPI PADDLING AGE RECORD: 87 YEARS OLD

Dale "Grey Beard" Sanders (87) set off from Lake Itasca on June 14 and reached Mile Marker Zero 87 days later, on September 7. This was the first official Guinness World Record for this category of paddling the Mississippi River.

2023, 8TH GUINNESS RECORD: 16 DAYS, 20 HOURS, 16 MINUTES

Scott Miller (47), Judson Steinback (42), Paul Cox (53), and Wally Werderich (50) set the Guinness World Record of 16 days, 20 hours, and 16 minutes from May 10. Their run had on-water support craft and was characterized by good weather and water conditions, and few lock-dam delays. A more detailed account can be found in the chapter "A Race for Redemption."

APPENDIX B

Cold Water Danger: A Lesson

Since March of 2021, when I was saved from a cold water drowning by a stroke of luck (see "Dead Cold"), I've tried to use my good fortune to help others see the danger that cold water poses. I've especially tried to reach people like myself, who knew this, but didn't really *get* it. After all, cold water doesn't look dangerous. It looks the same as it does all summer.

Many people aren't as lucky as I was. I read about these cases every year. In May of 2020, three young men were camping on Tuscarora Lake in the Boundary Waters when a gust of wind tipped their canoe. Two of them made it to shore, but Billy Cameron, twenty-nine, did not, even though he was wearing a life jacket.

On Memorial Day of 2021, a fifty-one-year-old man fell out of his boat while fishing on Trout Lake in the Boundary Waters. He was not wearing a life jacket, sank quickly in the cold water, and died.

In May of 2022, a forty-three-year-old paddler named Dave Kasprak, who had been to the BWCA some twenty times, took a solo trip on the Frost River in the eastern Boundary Waters. The banks were still lined with snow. The water was at record high levels. He told Minnesota Public Radio that he was "more intrigued by the conditions than fearful of them."

On his first day, a strong current flipped his canoe on Ham Lake. The current then pushed him further out, but he swam for shore pulling his canoe. It took him an hour to make it. His legs "started going numb and tingly."

After emptying his boat onshore, he paddled back to the portage, which was covered by a raging river. There he saw one of his food packs in the water and decided to try to grab it, but the current caught him and sent him downstream, which he said was "like getting beaten with bats going down a waterslide."

Kasprak managed to grab a branch on his way down the chute. When he pulled himself out of the water, he said: "I was shaking, beyond cold. I can't describe the kind of cold. It wasn't even cold anymore. It was like burning."

He took off his clothes, wrapped himself in a tarp, vomited, and passed out. When he woke up, he made camp. In the morning he hiked cross-country back to his car. He was almost as lucky as I was.

Water in the far north can be extremely cold into June. And according to the Cook County Sheriff's Department, it's cold all year. "Our stance," a representative said in an email, "is that all waters in northern Minnesota are considered 'cold water' no matter the time of year. Although the surface temperature can reflect 75 degrees, the water only a few feet down can be significantly colder."

* * *

Cold water drownings are different from warm water drownings. In cold water, it becomes hard to disentangle drowning and hypothermia, because they work in tandem. According to Minnesota Sea Grant director John A. Downing, "In the Great Lakes states, 35% more people die of hypothermia than drown, and many of those drowning deaths are due to exhaustion from hypothermia."

Cold water drownings can happen very fast, especially without a life jacket. The National Center for Cold Water Safety puts it bluntly: "Cold water is a predator—fast, powerful and deadly, with unlimited energy and no need for sleep. A predator so perfectly camouflaged that you can stand right next to it and see absolutely nothing dangerous—just a sparkling invitation to get out on the water and have some fun."

Temperature matters. By some estimates, in water 70 to 80

degrees Fahrenheit, you'll be able to swim for two hours, and your time to exhaustion is seven to twelve hours. At 50 to 60 degrees, your maximum swim time is down to seventy-five minutes, and time to exhaustion is one to two hours. And at 32.5 to 40 degrees, you likely have zero to seven minutes of swim time, and time to exhaustion or unconsciousness is fifteen to thirty minutes. (Times are longer with a portable flotation device.)

The National Center for Cold Water Safety disputes these estimates and warns that they give people a false sense of security, because they understate how fast manual dexterity can be lost and incapacitation (as opposed to exhaustion) can arrive. "You actually have a desperate race against the clock, and every minute, you get progressively weaker."

* * *

The water I capsized in was forty-two degrees Fahrenheit. The water in the BWCA in the weeks after ice-out will likely be in that range. But you can also become hypothermic in much warmer water, if you are in it long enough for it to drag your body temperature below ninety-five degrees.

COLD WATER DANGER: FOUR STAGES

If you find yourself in cold water, here are the four stages you will go through. The colder it is, the faster they will progress.

1. Cold Shock

This is a very dangerous time, right when you go in the water, characterized by "uncontrollable hyperventilation" in the first one to five minutes. Many people inhale water, go under, and die in this stage. It's important to control your breathing and stay calm.

2. Swim Failure

The next stage is physical incapacitation caused by, as Downing writes, "rapid cooling of skin, nerves, and muscles that results in a rapid loss of dexterity, sense of touch, muscle strength and speed." The rate of loss depends on the temperature. According to the National Center for Cold Water Safety, in this stage "you can no longer control your arms, legs, hands and feet. When this happens, particularly in waves, you are very likely to drown." Some research shows that nearly half the people who drown in cold water are two meters away from safety.

3. Hypothermia

In this stage, your body temperature drops below ninety-five degrees, because your body is losing heat more quickly than it can generate it. This happens faster in the water than in the air. And it happens faster when you are swimming than floating. Pamela Doty, writing for the US Army on how to survive in cold water, notes that "any movement in cold water is going to deplete your body of heat 25–30 times faster than cold air." This stage can also see the onset of disorientation, lethargy, and cognitive problems.

4. Post-Rescue Collapse

Even after you get pulled out, you're not out of danger. While it's not well understood, many people when they're rescued experience an abrupt drop in blood pressure, loss of consciousness, or heart failure. It's important to seek medical attention immediately.

COLD WATER SURVIVAL: WHAT TO DO?

The best way to survive a cold water plunge is not to take one in the first place, and to wait for warmer weather. But what should you do if you find yourself in cold water?

1. Get out of the water—or get as much of yourself out as you can—to minimize heat loss. This could mean climbing onto a boat or cooler, for example.
2. Stay focused and determined. Panic and hopelessness will significantly reduce your chances of survival. Stay calm and control your breathing, especially in the initial stages of cold shock.
3. If you do have to go out in cold water, stay near shore, wear a dry suit, and get canoe stabilizers to attach to your boat.

4. One common guideline is the "1-10-1 Rule," created by Dr. Gordon Giesbrecht. It says you have one minute to get your breathing under control, ten minutes (or less) for self-rescue, and one hour before you become unconscious from hypothermia. The National Center for Cold Water Safety disputes this, calling it unscientific, unrealistic, and misleading. Instead, they say, hyperventilation can last up to five minutes and incapacitation (lack of movement) can start in just a few minutes. You could have much less than twelve minutes, depending on the water temperature and how your body reacts. The bottom line is you have to stay calm and get out of the water as soon as you can.

* * *

After my story was published in the *Star Tribune*, I got a flood of emails from people who read it and were moved by it. Some had lost loved ones. Others had watched strangers drown in cold water. And others had nearly lost their own lives.

But the letter that made me feel best was from a man who said, "Frank, appreciate your article about your near death experience. I wonder if, and realize we'll never know, but I wonder if you've saved mine."

I can only hope he's right, and there are more out there like him.

NOTES ON SOURCES

THE LOST HISTORY OF THE PAUL BUNYAN CANOE DERBY

I originally envisioned this story as a short, historical piece about the evolution of canoe racing in Minnesota. What was the Paul Bunyan Aquatennial Canoe Derby? When did it even happen? No one seemed to know much about it.

So I went to the Gale Library at the Minnesota Historical Society and asked for the clippings file, which didn't have much. I went to the Hennepin History Museum, which had more material, plus a history/summary of the Aquatennial written by Catherine Mitchell of the College of St. Catherine in 1989. But there were still many holes to fill.

Around this time, I was interviewing Bob O'Hara for a broader piece about canoeing in Minnesota. He mentioned that Emily Broderson, president of the Minnesota Canoe Association, had interviewed a surviving Paul Bunyan Canoe Derby racer.

I sent Broderson a note, and she emailed me her interview with Bill Smith and connected me with him. I also arranged to go to his home to do my own interview. Talking to Bill was a revelation. At ninety-two, he still remembered things so vividly and recalled so many details and personalities. After that, I knew I would have to focus on the derby.

Back at the Gale Library, I dove into the Historic Minneapolis Tribune, an amazing digital resource. While not perfect, it does let you search back to the early 1900s for specific terms, like "canoe derby," "canoe marathon," and so on. The archive includes the *Minneapolis Morning Tribune*, the *Sunday Journal*, the *Minneapolis Sunday Tribune*, the *Minneapolis Star*, and the *Minneapolis Star Journal*, all of which evolved into the *Star Tribune* (Minneapolis) and more recently the *Minnesota Star Tribune*.

From this database, I collected 643 news stories, along with 157 photos and items from other sources. I arranged these by year and read though them many times to reconstruct the events of each race from 1928 to 1964, as well as the earlier events in the 1910s.

There was little mention of the 1919 Mississippi Marathon in the Star Tribune Historic Archive, but I did find information about this race in the *Winona Republican-Herald* and the *Wabasha County Herald*. No one I talked to had ever heard of the race, or knew that, in a sense, it laid the groundwork for the derby.

While I was in the middle of this research, I got a note from Scott Miller, who has always been fascinated with the derby and dreamed of reviving it. He had been giving a talk at an assisted living facility in Maple Grove when one of the residents told him he'd raced in the derby. Miller connected me with Stan Droogsma, and I arranged to interview him as well.

After a short version of the derby history was published in the Minnesota Historical Society's *Minnesota History* magazine (Fall 2024), I received a note from Wayne Thompson informing me that his father, Harlow Thompson, derby runner-up in 1950 and winner in 1951, was ninety-nine years old and still quite lucid. We arranged for a Zoom interview, and I spoke to Harlow for about an hour. Afterward, Wayne said he learned more about the derby in that hour than he had in the previous seventy years. Some additional context and information came from Dave Cline's first-person account of racing the derby, titled *Which Way Bena? Navigating the 450-mile Aquatennial Canoe Derby, July 8–17, 1959* (N.p: n.p, [2015?]).

Much valuable information about the Tibbetts family, in the form of obituaries and genealogical information, was scanned and sent to me by Lilah Crow, executive director of the Itasca County Historical Society in Grand Rapids.

Those were the main sources of information about the Paul Bunyan Canoe Derby. I believe there are more photos and stories out there (for example, in the *Minneapolis Daily News*), but these have not yet been located. There are probably photos in people's drawers and albums.

The historical information about the evolution of canoes came from interviews with Jim Jones Jr., a master canoe builder and member of the Leech Lake Band of Ojibwe; Wayne Valliere, a master canoe builder and member of the Lac du Flambeau Band of Lake Superior Chippewa Indians; Erik Simula, a master canoe builder who learned the craft from Bunky Fairbanks of Ball Club in the 1990s; and Mark Neuzil, author of *Canoes: A Natural History in North America* (Minneapolis: University of Minnesota Press, 2016). The Treuer quotation is from "Inside the Birchbark Canoe," *American Craft* (Spring 2023). I also used Howard I. Chapelle and Edwin Tappan Adney's *The Bark Canoes and Skin Boats of North America* (Washington, DC: Smithsonian Institution Press, 1964), as well as interviews and news stories about the Lake Mendota canoes discovered by Tamara Thomsen.

JOURNEYS AND ADVENTURERS

I learned the information in these two sections through my own experience and reporting. "Blue Highways" originally appeared in *Minnesota Monthly* (May 2015) and was edited by Rachel Hutton. "Uncharted Waters" appeared in *Southwest: The Magazine* (October 2016), the inflight publication of Southwest Airlines, and was edited by Bradford Pearson. "Dead Cold" (March 28 and May 27, 2022) and "Never So Terrified: A Night at Sturgeon Narrows" (October 31, 2019) were originally published in the *Minneapolis Star Tribune* and were edited by Bob Timmons; I wrote the latter based on emails from and interviews with Attila Ray Dabasi, who approves this reprinting. "The Canoe-Less Portage" (September–

October 2019), "Let it Flow" (September–October 2023), and "The Call of the River" (March 2024) all appeared in *Minnesota Conservation Volunteer*, the magazine of the Minnesota Department of Natural Resources, and were edited by Keith Goetzman. Sources for materials added to the "The Canoe-Less Portage" include Carolyn Gilman's *The Grand Portage Story* (St. Paul: Minnesota Historical Society Press, 1992); the National Park Service's "Grand Portage: A History of The Sites, People, and Fur Trade" (https://npshistory.com/publications/grpo/history/chap1.htm); Douglas A. Birk's "Recent Underwater Recoveries at Fort Charlotte, Grand Portage National Monument, Minnesota," *International Journal of Nautical Archaeology and Underwater Exploration* 4, no. 1 (March 1975); and my own interview with Jerry Pushcar, author of *Waters Beneath My Feet* (Nome, AK: Last Cache Publishing, 2018).

THE RACE FOR THE RECORD

I learned the information in this section through my own reporting and experience. "An Epic Battle" was originally published at *Outside* magazine as "The Epic Battle to Break the Mississippi River Canoe Record" (November 2021) and was edited by Abigail Wise. Early drafts included my first-person experiences on the Mile Marker Zero support crew, but Abby wisely (no pun intended) cut those to make the story purely about the race. The first-person sections now appear here for the first time in "Crewing the Record."

"A Race for Redemption," originally titled "A Record-Breaking Paddle Down the Mississippi River," was also published at *Outside* and was edited by Frederick Dreier. The version that appears here is my original draft and wording.

APPENDICES

As noted, the information in "The History of the Mississippi Record" was largely gathered by former record holder Clark Eid and supplemented my own interview with Tim Muhich, as well as my participation with the Mile Marker Zero (2021) and Mississippi Speed

Record (2023) teams. It is printed here with Eid's permission. Clark is the keeper of much knowledge and many pieces of the past river records. At the time of this writing, these artifacts are in search of a museum to call home.

The story "Cold Water Danger" was originally published on the Friends of the Boundary Waters website and was edited by David Meier.

Frank Bures is a writer whose work has appeared in *Harper's, Outside*, *The Atlantic*, and many other publications. His stories have been included in *The Best American Travel Writing* anthologies and won other awards. He is the author of *The Geography of Madness*, editor of *Under Purple Skies*, and producer of audio history tours for VoiceMap. He grew up on the Mississippi River in Winona, Minnesota, and has lived in Italy, Tanzania, New Zealand, Thailand, and Wisconsin. He lives in Minneapolis, Minnesota. More at frankbures.com.